STREAMLINING the CURRICULUM

ASCD MEMBER BOOK

STREAMLINING the CURRICULUM

Using the Storyboard Approach to Frame Compelling Learning Journeys

Heidi Hayes Jacobs
Allison Zmuda

Arlington, Virginia USA

2800 Shirlington Road, Suite 1001 • Arlington, VA 22206 USA
Phone: 800-933-2723 or 703-578-9600 • Fax: 703-575-5400
Website: www.ascd.org • Email: member@ascd.org
Author guidelines: www.ascd.org/write

Richard Culatta, *Chief Executive Officer;* Anthony Rebora, *Chief Content Officer;* Genny Ostertag, *Managing Director, Book Acquisitions & Editing;* Mary Beth Nielsen, *Director, Book Editing;* Katie Martin, *Senior Editor;* Thomas Lytle, *Creative Director;* Donald Ely, *Art Director;* Georgia Park, *Senior Graphic Designer;* Cynthia Stock, *Typesetter;* Kelly Marshall, *Production Manager;* Shajuan Martin, *E-Publishing Specialist;* Christopher Logan, *Senior Production Specialist*

PAPERBACK ISBN: 978-1-4166-3220-7 ASCD product #123020
PDF EBOOK ISBN: 978-1-4166-3221-4; see Books in Print for other formats.
Quantity discounts are available: email programteam@ascd.org or call 800-933-2723, ext. 5773, or 703-575-5773. For desk copies, go to www.ascd.org/deskcopy.

ASCD Member Book No. F23-10 (Sep. 2023 PSI+). ASCD Member Books mail to Premium (P), Select (S), and Institutional Plus (I+) members on this schedule: Jan, PSI+; Feb, P; Apr, PSI+; May, P; Jul, PSI+; Aug, P; Sep, PSI+; Nov, PSI+; Dec, P. For current details on membership, see www.ascd.org/membership.

Library of Congress Cataloging-in-Publication Data

Names: Jacobs, Heidi Hayes, author. | Zmuda, Allison, author.
Title: Streamlining the curriculum : using the storyboard approach to frame compelling learning journeys / Heidi Hayes Jacobs, Allison Zmuda.
Description: Arlington, Virginia, USA : ASCD, [2023] | Includes bibliographical references and index.
Identifiers: LCCN 2023014486 (print) | LCCN 2023014487 (ebook) | ISBN 9781416632207 (paperback) | ISBN 9781416632214 (pdf)
Subjects: LCSH: Teacher participation in curriculum planning—United States. | Curriculum planning—United States. | Storyboards—United States. | Effective teaching—United States. | Motivation in education.
Classification: LCC LB2806.15 .J335 2023 (print) | LCC LB2806.15 (ebook) | DDC 375/.001—dc23/eng/20230405
LC record available at https://lccn.loc.gov/2023014486
LC ebook record available at https://lccn.loc.gov/2023014487

32 31 30 29 28 27 26 25 24 23 1 2 3 4 5 6 7 8 9 10 11 12

With love, gratitude, and admiration,
we dedicate this book to Bena Kallick.
A gifted storyteller with a listening ear,
Bena makes learning wondrous. As a keen
observer with an unerring grasp of the human
experience, she leads gently and courageously.
With boundless optimism, she exudes a
perpetual openness to fresh thinking.

Streamlining the Curriculum

Prologue

Meet Alicia, a teacher who began her career optimistic about teaching young people to explore the world through the questions they investigated and the creations they made. But over the years, Alicia has found that the curriculum expectations keep her—and her students—working at a pace too relentless for exploration. She spends hours searching on websites and chat boards, trying to figure out how to get her students interested in what she's required to teach them.

Meet Sam, a school leader who has grown weary of trying to motivate his colleagues to design a curriculum that is both standards-aligned and meaningful to the students. His efforts are met with quiet resistance, even as teachers diligently fill out the curriculum form according to his directions. Now Sam spends hours searching on websites and chat boards, trying to figure out how to jump-start a school culture that values deep inquiry and authentic learning experiences. If only he could get his colleagues to circle back and take this curriculum redesign opportunity seriously.

Now meet a few students. First, there is 6-year-old Iris, who had once been eager to conquer consonant blends and diphthongs but is now feeling defeated as the rest of her reading group races through letters and sound patterns and the leveled books. And then there's Max, a sophomore who beelines to the back row of every classroom. He has been keeping a low profile since middle school and long ago disconnected from daily planned learning experiences, which just don't interest him much. Max likes many of his teachers but notices that they seem to be teaching on a treadmill, speaking faster and faster at the end of class, trying to "fit it all in" before the bell rings.

Schooling is often compared to a journey—one in which learners face challenges, confront problems, acquire skills, build understanding, and develop wisdom. But when learners have little or no say in their schooling's direction, are they really the heroes of this journey? Is the journey "theirs"? Is it even a journey at all?

The Challenges We Face . . . and the Opportunity It Offers

The curriculum as it currently stands is untenable, bloated, overly detailed, and uninspiring. As teachers like Alicia scan their classrooms, they see young faces resigned to the fact that the topics they are most interested in and fascinated by will not be part of the day's agenda. Educators have made this problem worse with design templates we insist on as best practice even though they are dysfunctional for the end user: teachers.

Teachers and school leaders have an enormous stake in the schooling journey—and an opportunity, should we rise to it, to reexamine the content foundations of our curriculum and unearth a compelling narrative thread to help shape the journey our students are on. The solution we propose is a fresh way of telling a curriculum story. It's one that calls upon educators to take on a collection of roles that may be unfamiliar:

- *Creative writer,* imagining narrative threads that capture the heart of the content and the imagination of the students.
- *Editor,* examining what is realistic given the time frame of a school year and making the necessary cuts and consolidations.
- *Composer,* focusing on how multiple audiences will connect with the narrative and providing a clear and succinct snapshot of the overall experience that coordinates with the school community.
- *Networker,* opening opportunities for learners to connect with the issues, ideas, and people they find fascinating.

As educators begin to see ourselves in these interconnected roles, our curriculum documents can become lanterns, lighting the way for the kind of heroic exploration that led most of us to teaching in the first place and allowing us to pursue wonderment alongside our students. Grappling with the issues of overwhelming curriculum documents and demands—and of disengaged, passive students—and producing practical options for action are the core of this book. To that end, we propose to expand the approach and modernize the forms used to capture and develop meaningful learning experiences.

For decades, the two of us have been fascinated by curriculum development. Heidi launched her writing career with *Interdisciplinary Curriculum: Design and Implementation* (Jacobs, 1989) and went on to develop the concept of *curriculum mapping* and pioneer both the curriculum mapping model as well as the modernization of learning environments. Allison began her writing career with *The Competent Classroom* (Zmuda & Tomaino, 2001), laying out a homegrown curriculum design influenced by Grant Wiggins and Jay McTighe (2005). Her work with Understanding by Design, paired with her commitment to personalized learning, grew her belief in students as powerful partners in learning. Developing and using curriculum to imagine, organize, and refine learning plans became the heart of our individual work as consultants, authors, and thought partners.

As close friends and colleagues, we have regularly explored questions about curriculum design; in recent years, we have become deeply attuned to the *effect* of that design on the end user. In fall 2019, our first "writing sketches"—collaborative journal entries that documented our early conversations—were peppered with lines like these:

- *The toll that pacing guides and expectations takes on students? Heartbreaking for learners.*
- *Curriculum has become a rutted path versus a well-worn track—hardened, difficult to travel.*
- *Balking at the "path to run"—student fatigue.*
- *The tyranny of templates and aggressive pacing guides. Losing connections, relationships, content, relevance.*
- *We are the stewards of our own learning.*
- *Using a narrative arc to build immersion—attention and emotional resonance. Beginning, middle, end—the next adventure gets you excited.*
- *Lean into what is possible, interesting, worthwhile, challenging, doable, into what has meaning and emotional resonance.*
- *Link to pedagogy—students as story makers and storytellers.*

What emerged in our early writing days was a reckoning that we all had gone a bit astray in our focus on unit and course development. Much of what we have done has inadvertently perpetuated an antiquated curricular path. And we own that. We started to think about learning as an invitation to a journey where our heroes—our students—are cast in the roles of narrator and protagonist.

Our early flow resembled a three-act play, with each act moving the narrative forward:

- Act 1 was a statement of purpose and exploration of the hero's challenge. We asked, *What's the problem that will drive the learning journey?*
- In Act 2, we delved deeper into the metaphor of learning as the kind of hero's journey found in epic poetry and stories and thought more about the learner's experience. We asked, *What obstacles will learners encounter? What allies and adversaries will they interact with along the way? What will they be learning or seeing for the first time? What will they be learning or seeing in a new light?*
- In Act 3, we considered the options and approaches that might naturally emerge to motivate learners, which helped us unpack the hero's growth. We asked, *What will students learn with this approach? How might learning in this way change them? What tools and approaches will they take forward?*

When the two of us, Heidi and Allison, began breaking out of curriculum template shackles, we became fascinated with a phenomena-based approach at the heart of Acts 2 and 3. We developed a model and were excited to prototype it at the 2020 ASCD Annual Conference. Then COVID-19 hit in March 2020. Suddenly, students were out of school and at home behind screens, and teachers were scrambling to develop and teach lessons using largely unfamiliar digital platforms and tools. Heidi received the following urgent call from a director of magnet programs in a northeastern U.S. city:

> What are we going to do? All our schools will close on site; starting next week, every teacher will need to work remotely with their students. What I'm worried about is how we will be able to communicate with the kids and the parents who will struggle to follow the list of tasks, activities, and resources in a packed curriculum. Our teachers are asking for a simplified curricular approach in manageable chunks for lesson planning.

Educators across the globe can identify with these concerns. In April of that same year, we interviewed the primary and secondary principals of Hong Kong International School; they noted that when their school first went into lockdown mode during the Hong Kong riots in November 2019, they were startled by how crucial it was to change the approach they were using. Teachers with the best of intentions were sending home packed schedules of activities written in a wide range of idiosyncratic styles, making it difficult for families to decipher. (Our 2021 article in *Educational Leadership,* titled "Streamlined Lesson Planning for Learner Engagement," takes a closer look at these events.) The principals realized that the school needed to communicate in language that reached parents and learners.

But the pandemic also brought a larger, long-brewing issue to the foreground—the jam-packed nature of our curriculum. Every year we add more content to the annual maps while taking little away. The sheer size of the curriculum can push teachers into a claustrophobic corner where coverage is their only way out. Thus, even if they had a fresh approach to lesson planning, teachers would still be hindered by unit pile-on. *There's always more information to dispense, and there are always more tests to administer.* When teacher reserves are depleted, it's hard to enthusiastically engage in teaching and learning. And then there's that gnawing sense of what is really driving decisions about what can and should be taught: the end-of-year test.

So how do we get out from under these burdens? How do we make choices about what matters most? How do we move away from the coverage approach to direct engagement? We can do this by streamlining the curriculum so that it provides clarity, relevance, and engagement.

The Promise of Streamlining

The *Merriam-Webster Dictionary* (n.d.) defines *streamline* as "to bring up to date: modernize; to put in order: organize; to make simpler or more efficient." The *Online Etymology Dictionary* (n.d.) identifies the word as originating in the field of hydraulics and meaning "free from turbulence." In business, *streamlining* refers to the process of simplifying or eliminating unnecessary work-related tasks to improve efficiency.

In the most fundamental terms, streamlining curriculum makes learning easier to access, understand, and use; it also makes the curriculum more effective, engaging, purposeful, timely, and connected. Whenever we share this concept with audiences, heads immediately nod in agreement. Streamlining simply makes things work better.

The lessons we learned from the pandemic propelled us to shift away from our habitual curriculum design practices to a fresh approach. Here are five recurring themes running throughout this book:

1. **Moving from cumbersome and officious formats and templates to more streamlined versions.** Templates need to be easy to use, understand, and communicate to the target audience; they should include visual cues and accessible language. People will use what is usable.
2. **Moving from making curriculum content in pacing guides the focus of learning to making curriculum decisions based on learner roles.** We support regular editorial reviews to address what to cut out in the curriculum, what to cut back, what to consolidate, and what to create. These decisions should be guided by the aspirations we have for students framed as school or district student goals. This humanizes learning by inviting students into the curriculum story so they can better make connections, predictions, and extensions for future learning.
3. **Moving from "covering" the curriculum to developing a narrative approach to writing curriculum storyboards across the school year.** When we say a "narrative approach," we're referring to curriculum being developed as a deliberate throughline that identifies connected experiences in storytelling form. We use a curriculum storyboard to plot out a visual map sequencing the units of a course to share the learning journey with students. It shows them where they're going, the major stops along the way, and the various learner roles they will take on—for example, as investigator, researcher, or historian. Students make explicit connections as they actively interpret the story so far, make predictions, and raise personal inquiries on their journey. It's also a neuro-friendly way to frame learning. We will explore key neuroscience findings that align with this design practice later on in the book.
4. **Moving from detailed instructional plans written in teacher-facing language to a narrative approach to writing learning sets on the level of the lesson plan.** Here we extend the principles of narrative to

the daily and weekly lesson plan. The learning set model replaces old-style lesson planning and communicates directly with students and their families. (For an example of a learning set that we created for you, our readers, see the Learning Set Table of Contents on pp. 9–12.)

5. **Moving from a rigid, static, and calcified curriculum to a revitalized curriculum that captures emergent learning.** Integrating relevant events, problems, and issues in the world of our students breathes life into the curriculum. Teachers must not only make instructional and planning changes, but also help students identify and pitch possibilities for new learning. Guiding students in developing their narratives supports their academic strength even as it humanizes the classroom by cultivating a sense of belonging.

A Partnership for Composing Curriculum

Developing a coherent narrative—a curriculum—is a courageous and creative act of laying out possibilities and being willing to cut out, cut back, and consolidate ideas. You might cut hundreds of pages. You might scrap dozens of ideas while reexamining how to approach standard topics to best promote students' thinking and encourage them to take action.

In such a curriculum, students assume the roles of investigator, curator, innovator, and designer; they become more skillful and sophisticated in the questions they ask, the creations they produce, and the networks they engage in to better understand. You will need to reserve space for the emergent—for the unexpected issues, ideas, and events that students are energized to talk about and pursue. Learning in this capacity feels wildly fresh because it emerged from the grassroots level. In the absence of such a focus, even the best curriculum narratives can become stale. An engaging curriculum needs room to breathe.

Students can also cocreate or even take the lead in designing this type of curriculum. They capture their thinking, which results in the next choice on the journey. They ask themselves questions like these: *What am I finding along the way? What fascinates me? What no longer holds my interest? How have I gotten more knowledgeable and skillful? In what ways have I become more confused, having recognized the complexity of a topic or examined multiple perspectives?* Such an approach to learning is far healthier than going after a grade. Leaders provide the space to create responsive inspired learning experiences even as they weave in the power of purposeful standards and goals. Their role is analogous to a publisher who adheres to editorial standards but develops a wide-ranging catalogue.

How to Read This Book

We're providing two ways to organize your reading experience. The first is laid out in the traditional table of contents, where you'll find the title and focus of each of this book's chapters. The second one, the Learning Set Table of Contents, appears after this Prologue on pages 9–12 and models the concept of curriculum narrative in reader-facing language. The learning set model we're using is based on the same model we initially developed to streamline lesson planning. The intention behind this is simply to practice what we preach—activating you, the reader, as navigator, curator, and creator throughout this curriculum journey.

From this point on, we'll refer to the chapters as *episodes*. Each starts out by highlighting a learning target and three action verbs—*engage, examine,* and *act;* these frame what we intend you to engage with and examine as you make your way through the text and the possible actions you might take. Each episode is part of a larger story of how to streamline and guide narrative choices to develop a fresh, inviting journey for learners. Note that the Learning Set Table of Contents includes essential questions, overarching goals, and synopses of all 12 episodes.

You will see iconography used throughout the book to highlight the action verbs we use to frame your learning experience:

Engage

Examine

Act

We've also woven in perspectives and language for designing experiences from a range of fields. Whether employing approaches from a choreographer's notebook, an entrepreneur's marketing plan, or an anthropologist's ethnographic study, we hope to model multiple ways to reimagine the curriculum. The heroes in the schooling journey—every individual student, their teachers, and school leaders—need and deserve an empowering resolution.

TITLE	*Streamlining the Curriculum* by Heidi Hayes Jacobs and Allison Zmuda

Essential Question(s)

- *How can we shed and replace burdensome templates that drain energy?*
- *How can we streamline curriculum to make it compelling and actionable for our contemporary learners?*

Overarching Goal(s)

- *Streamline our curriculum design practices to engage students in timely, relevant experiences*

Overview—Prologue

We make the case for streamlining curriculum to replace dated planning practices and to directly engage modern learners. An editorial stance informs curricular decisions about what to cut out, cut back, consolidate, and create. We advocate for the development of curriculum as a narrative, using a storyboarding approach across the school year and daily. The heart of this approach is to create space for capturing emergent learning that humanizes and revitalizes the narrative for students on their journey.

Learning Target	Engage	Examine	Act
Episode 1: Breaking Free from the Tyranny of Templates We can evaluate the need for streamlining curriculum templates to increase their effectiveness and ease of use and better engage our learners.	Probe the problems that ensue from cumbersome curriculum templates and formats.	Analyze examples of problematic templates and their effect on teachers and learners.	Identify the degree to which your curriculum needs streamlining for end users.
Learning Target	**Engage**	**Examine**	**Act**
Episode 2: Using Modern Learner Roles to Streamline the Curriculum We can leverage modern learner roles to streamline curriculum narratives and corresponding assessments.	Consider how modern learner roles affect streamlining choices, curriculum narratives, and assessment designs.	Review case studies of mission statements converted into learner roles, as well as their effect on the learner's experience.	Draft learner roles based on mission and vision to focus curriculum narratives and assessment designs.

Learning Target	Engage	Examine	Act
Episode 3: What to Cut Out, Cut Back, Consolidate, and Create We can streamline our curriculum by making thoughtful choices about what it contains.	Explore how the editorial stance leads to effective curriculum streamlining.	Analyze examples from schools that have streamlined curriculum in three ways: in a disciplinary, an interdisciplinary, and a phenomena-based setting.	Make choices about what to cut out, cut back, consolidate, and create at a system or classroom level.
Episode 4: The Power of a Storyline We can compose curriculum as a narrative to engage learners in identifying meaningful connections.	Explore why curriculum framed as narrative is more memorable for students.	Model what curriculum narratives look like using two storyboard examples.	Review and reflect on current curriculum plans to generate possibilities.
Episode 5: Using the Setting to Streamline the Narrative We can select the setting to frame the curriculum narrative.	Explore framing the setting using a disciplinary, an interdisciplinary, and a phenomena-based curricular approach.	Analyze and reflect on how varied curricular settings can open up fresh possibilities.	Identify opportunities to reframe the storyline using a blend of disciplinary, interdisciplinary, and phenomena-based settings.
Episode 6: Genre Selection: Sketching a Course and Unit Narrative We can generate fresh curriculum possibilities through genre selection in course and unit design.	Look at the effect on curriculum of various genre choices: topics, themes, problems, issues, and case studies.	Analyze genre selections and their effect on content in disciplinary, interdisciplinary, and phenomena-based settings.	Develop fresh possibilities through genre selection and streamline the curriculum content.

Learning Target	Engage	Examine	Act
Episode 7: How Authentic Assessments Bolster the Curriculum Narrative We can develop authentic assessments to make a curriculum narrative come alive for learners.	Explore four criteria for authentic assessment.	Examine examples of authentic assessments that enliven the curriculum narrative.	Identify places in the curriculum narrative best suited for authentic assessments and sketch out ideas.
Episode 8: Generating a Curriculum Storyboard We can draft a storyboard narrative for a course using compositional choices to ensure learner engagement.	Explore elements and tips that will help in drafting an engaging storyboard.	Peruse examples of storyboards to consider which elements to include and to aid in drafting a course narrative.	Draft a storyboard narrative for a course using compositional choices.
Episode 9: Implementing Storyboards We can implement storyboarding by connecting with our learners, mapping within our system, and in daily planning.	Connect streamlining and using the storyboard approach with existing practices to amplify impact.	Examine storyboard implementation strategies via engaging instructional prompts, systemwide unit and mapping, and daily planning through learning sets.	Draft learning sets for specific learners, and streamline teacher planning time. Design prompts to encourage student interaction with storyboards and draft learning sets.
Episode 10: Framing Emergent Narratives We can pursue emergent narratives to keep curriculum vital and relevant.	Explore the origins and nature of emergent narratives and the use of the pitch-to-pitch model.	Analyze examples of teacher- and student-generated emergent narratives in curriculum.	Identify strategies and approaches to developing emergent learning opportunities.

Learning Target	Engage	Examine	Act
Episode 11: Student-Initiated Storyboards: We can help students create and fulfill their own learning narratives.	Explore how students can launch a meaningful pitch leading to a storyboard narrative.	Examine the four-phase pitch-to-pitch model to design a student narrative.	Craft a storyboard template to capture the student-led narrative, seeking opportunities for implementation.

Learning Target	Engage	Examine	Act
Episode 12: Sharing Curriculum Narratives with Families We can communicate curriculum narratives to families to promote connection.	Explore the need for transparency and connection in sharing curriculum with families.	Review examples to identify the applicability and value to your classroom and school practices of sharing curriculum with families.	Create or revise family curriculum communications.

Epilogue

Episode 1

Breaking Free from the Tyranny of Templates

Learning Target	Engage	Examine	Act
We can evaluate the need for streamlining curriculum templates to increase their effectiveness and ease of use and better engage our learners.	Probe the problems that ensue from cumbersome curriculum templates and formats.	Analyze examples of problematic templates and their effect on teachers and learners.	Identify the degree to which your curriculum needs streamlining for end users.

ENGAGE

An elementary school teacher is balancing multiple subjects and a roomful of 2nd graders; a high school teacher has 180 students and 3 preps. For teachers like these, overpacked and out-of-touch curriculum pacing guides, coupled with having to fill out cumbersome unit and lesson templates, prove exhausting.

The templates are a big part of the problem. You are no doubt familiar with them; they're packed with granular entries in six-point type that list the criteria needed to reach a subhead from a standard. Something is wrong when it takes more time to fill out unit planning forms than it does to decide on what students will actually do in class on a day-to-day basis. Lacking clarity, students find themselves caught up in a whirlwind of content, struggling to catch their breath long enough to learn what a decimal is, figure out why there is a periodic table of the elements, or recall what Abraham Lincoln said at Gettysburg.

Education is not the only field in which templates play a role in communication and creation. Consider, for example, the consistency and simplicity of the templates used in the fields of music and architecture. Although the complexity, range, and richness of musical works and architectural structures have truly evolved and expanded, the templates used—musical notation and blueprints—have remained remarkably the same. There are no labored and lengthy additions. Mozart used the same schema in his compositions that contemporary American composer Philip Glass has used in his. Nor do we expect the templates in music and architecture to be the thing itself. The musical notes of a score are symbolic representations on paper of what musicians will later create. Likewise, a blueprint doesn't capture all of what the building will become—how it might soar to the sky or inspire reverence. And yet any architect can make sense of the blueprint, just as any trained pianist can play sheet music. Why? Because the templates are easy to follow. In short, they are *streamlined.* They are simple but not simplistic.

Or take the field of industrial design, with its focus on form and function. During the 20th century, one of the greatest advocates for streamlining product design was Henry Dreyfuss. We see his prolific design contributions throughout our homes and offices, in our thermostats, telephones, and Hoover vacuum cleaners. Here's how Dreyfuss (1955) defined his design philosophy:

> We bear in mind that the object being worked on is going to be ridden in, sat upon, looked at, talked into, activated, operated, or in some other way *used by people*. When the point of contact between the product and the people becomes a point of friction, then the industrial designer has failed. On the other hand, if people are made safer, more efficient, more comfortable—or just plain happier—by contact with the product, then the designer has succeeded. (pp. 25–26)

Think of the curriculum document you follow. Ask yourself, *What is its purpose? Who uses it?* In our experience, if a curriculum document is list upon list of standards and substandards, it's barely read at all. Or readers will simply cherry-pick. It becomes what Dreyfuss refers to as "a point of friction." Filling out a curriculum template that is neither helpful for teachers nor effective for students results in what we call *unit fatigue*. But there is an upside to this—it can trigger the creation of an easy-to-use format that will lighten teachers' loads. Ask yourself what you need to cut, what you need to consolidate, and what you need to create in the template itself.

A school needs to own the template it uses when laying out curriculum. Faculty members need to review those templates and figure out how to transform them into useful tools capable of constructing strong unit and lesson plans. Setting aside time for this examination is a worthy investment.

EXAMINE

The complexity and onslaught of state- and district-level documents are prime culprits. They're often embedded in institutions, and they're seldom checked for efficiency or effective design. Do these forms actually reveal what we value—or do they perpetuate a system at odds with our educational purpose? The intention of state, provincial, and national guiding overview documents is always to assist, yet they tend to be long, detailed lists of outcomes for each grade in each subject without calibration regarding timing. Sometimes the various governmental education websites post standards, curriculum documents, or pacing guides packed with worthwhile resources, but they are difficult to translate to a school's program, let alone guide a classroom teacher.

Consider the purpose and format of standards. Standards are taxonomies. They are long lists of proficiency targets organized under categories in grade or age-level spans. Their intended purpose is to describe granular competencies that will be translated into curriculum that teachers will develop and that learners will ultimately demonstrate. Standards are not written to be curriculum friendly; they're not teacher friendly, and they're certainly not student friendly. Yes, they are important and can serve as a ballast to quality teaching and learning, but school faculties spend far too much time unpacking them, figuring out what each of them means, and converting them into the lived experience of the classroom.

And what happens in the meantime? *A living, breathing curriculum can get lost because the reader is lost.* Perhaps this is the reveal. If teachers must spend so much time and energy to get through oversight documents, then the aim is compliance, not creative learning designs. So most teachers roll up their sleeves and do the best they can to make sense of their grade- or course-level assignments without attending to the vertical effect of their curriculum choices on their colleagues. And within their horizontal unit design choices, the pacing plans become strenuous for both teachers and learners, taking out the very juice that makes the curriculum alive.

Here are some questions to ask yourself:

- Based on where you live, what do the external standards prioritize or value?
- To what extent do the related standardized measures align with what is prioritized or valued?
- To what extent is achieving the standards feasible? Do you have enough time and space for student inquiry and authentic tasks?
- To what extent is there flexibility in how local schools and individual teachers can frame their learning designs?

Unit Templates

Unit templates typically show how external curriculum standards align with assessment, describe key content and skills, and reflect instructional practice. They have the best of intentions, but they frequently go awry. These templates start by laying out the basics: unit title or theme, grade and subject, and time frame. But they often require detailed descriptions and overviews, along with a list of applicable content standards, key objectives, and core vocabulary words. Perhaps they need to reference a school's broader goals, such as its Portrait of a Graduate statement, or various essential questions and understandings. As curriculum designers dutifully fill in each of these components, the template typically will span two to four pages just to articulate the learning goals.

As they move to create summative and formative assessments, curriculum designers often experience *design amnesia*. The flood of entries in the learning goals can make it difficult to measure what matters, especially when "what matters most" is a multipage explanation. Not only will the assessments tend to be misaligned with the learning goals, but the weariness of the designers may affect their enthusiasm for developing authentic and meaningful assessments.

When they finally focus on the instructional plan, curriculum designers are typically exhausted and may simply want to identify resources, list instructional materials from a textbook or program, or provide a general outline of topics and let teachers fend for themselves. Although this information may be helpful, the teachers still have to do the heavy lift of making sense of these resources and materials to develop actionable teaching and learning plans. As a California independent school curriculum director put it,

> Our teachers have had it by spending the few professional days we have available sifting through long lists of standards and then filling out overly detailed unit plans. They know they need to have unit goals, key questions for inquiry, and learning standards, but isn't there a way to make this easier? They feel they never get to the direct planning of learning experiences. (Personal communication, July 2021).

Many curriculum designers, as they're drafting, grumble about the audience for this work. They want to know *who* they're writing for exactly—for their supervisor to evaluate their performance? For administrators to share with the community? For an external audit that checks for alignment to what the governmental or international organization values? Rarely do curriculum designers believe that developing ideas in the template will affect what and how teachers actually teach.

Consider the effect on curriculum design if we were to address fundamental questions such as these:

- Who is the audience for the unit template?
- How will teachers use it?

- Is it easy to use?
- To what extent does it clarify what is mandated and where teachers have some flexibility?
- To what extent does it regularly include contemporary, authentic, and challenging tasks?

Lesson Plan Templates

Developing a lesson plan template is a promising opportunity for teachers to create an effective and engaging learning sequence that demonstrates their knowledge of their students, curriculum, and pedagogy. Teachers can also share their lesson plans. Such plans can provide valuable guidance for short- or long-term substitute teachers, as well as documentation for administrators to use in teacher evaluation.

But the reality is that teachers often view the exercise as a bureaucratic endeavor that has limited value in developing their professional expertise. Typical lesson plan templates ask for clarification on the topic and lesson outcomes, as well as a breakdown of lesson structure (time and focus); related resources and materials; and how teachers will assess the learning. Once teachers submit the plans, building administrators often struggle with what to do with them, outside of preparing for a formal teacher evaluation. Theoretically, administrators *could* use them to examine current instructional practice across grade-level teams, departments, or schools in service to desired schoolwide outcomes. However, many administrators already have so much on their plate, not to mention the weariness of the teachers who are expected to develop the lesson plan templates and the weariness of the administrators who are expected to review them. And we still haven't drilled down to the students yet.

Consider the effect on lesson templates and tools if curriculum developers asked questions like these:

- Who is the audience for the lesson plan?
- How will teachers use it?
- To what extent does it promote more focused conversations about pedagogy?
- To what extent does it regularly include contemporary, authentic, and challenging learning experiences?

We believe that formats should be simplified to support a *literal curriculum narrative* that is accessible and engaging to learners. In our subsequent episodes, we will be looking at a fresh design approach: *narrative storyboards* and *learning sets.*

ACT

Before heading into areas where educators have more locus of control, we want to first acknowledge the broader picture.

Streamlining at the Systems Level

In terms of district, state, provincial, or national levels, let us begin by loosening the knots that tie us to unwieldy documents. We advocate a fundamental design shift in the *format, purpose, accessibility,* and *audience* for big-picture perspective documents. Although it may seem daunting to streamline state, provincial, and national curriculum standards, two models are helpful here.

First, the national curriculum of Australia (Australian Curriculum, Assessment, and Reporting Authority, 2022) has a streamlined set of guidelines that are easy to navigate and provide stimulating resources for building purposeful learning experiences. Each subject is easy to access at any level, from Foundations through Year 10 (F–10). Within subjects, the tabs and curricular headers are simple and clear, and they naturally suit the subject, while also providing cross-disciplinary applications if a teacher wishes to develop those as well. They are written in plain English—Year, Strands, General Capabilities, and Cross-Disciplinary Priorities—as opposed to more convoluted educationese. For example, when opening up General Capabilities, which are akin to standards that we see in the United States, you will find seven boxes: critical and creative thinking, digital literacy, ethical understanding, intercultural understanding, literacy, numeracy, and personal and social capability. These showcase key inquiry questions to assist teachers, as well as sample student portfolio items that reflect more complex and higher-order assessments. *The site is clearly designed to go straight into the hands of teachers.*

The second example comes from Finland. We had the opportunity to meet one of the leaders of the Finnish reform movement, Irmelina Halinen. She made a point of traveling throughout Finland with her research teams interviewing students about school and learning to inform their recommendations for the proposed curricular reform. Halinen (2018) writes about the importance of the student in the curriculum:

> From the learners' point of view, the focus of the reform was to improve the joy and meaningfulness of learning and student agency, enhancing thinking and learning to learn as well as other transversal skills, and to support the development of schools as collaborative learning communities. An integrative, multidisciplinary pedagogical approach was emphasized, and new tools for crossing the boundaries of subjects were developed. (p. 80)

This commitment points to ensuring there is time and space to breathe in the curriculum and that local schools have discretion to adjust the curriculum in response to their specific learners. It positions teachers to "have more professional autonomy" (p. 245).

It may seem that educators have little influence over the decisions made at this level. Yet policy decisions are primarily driven by the needs of the constituents these organizations serve. Key is a respect for and investment in professionals. As Pasi Sahlberg (2015) notes, "The key word between teachers and authorities in Finland is *trust.* Indeed, professional autonomy requires trust, and trust makes teacher autonomy alive" (para. 18).

We do recognize that these systemic shifts may take time. Nevertheless, schools and districts can take action in the interim.

What Schools and Districts *Can* Control

Ultimately, we're advocating for what is actionable with students and teachers in schools. The following suggestions can assist in unit and lesson design.

Evaluate the extent to which course, unit, and lesson templates need streamlining.

Begin a streamlined approach using the following prompts:

- What would teachers find useful from a system's perspective to develop a robust and modern curriculum?

- What might that template look like at the program, course, unit, and lesson levels?
- What could we shed that is unnecessary, redundant, and distracting in our current documents?

Having clear and streamlined templates will help teachers curb their tendency to "cover" the curriculum. A focus on determining the elements required to convey crucial points on the pathway can help district and systemwide organizations revise their planning documents. This would loosen up aggressive pacing guides, scope and sequence charts, and overly detailed unit and lesson plans.

Clarify the priorities for and with your curriculum designers.

Sometimes the templates are reasonable, but the expectations for curriculum designers are unclear or unfeasible. The goal is usability. Consider the following questions:

- To what extent does the template clearly define the unit and lesson components? Creating a glossary of terms, as well as quality criteria, can guide the development of units and lessons.
- To what extent is the intended audience—teachers—at the forefront of administrators' and curriculum designers' minds in articulating units and lessons? Having empathy for the end users not only helps with streamlining the content but also opens up more breathing room at the classroom level for personalizing learning based on needs, interests, and emergent issues.
- To what extent is there a continued commitment to revise unit and lesson plans? Revisiting general expectations and timelines with curriculum designers and administrators helps highlight priorities in the revision and clarifies how to organize a quality review process that focuses on those priorities. Such priorities might be strengthening horizontal and vertical coherence, developing tasks to amplify learner engagement, integrating innovative tools, and consistently using specific schoolwide instructional practices.

Consider grade-level bands and teacher looping to promote connections.

The notion of the academic year may be a culprit in overpacking the curriculum, given the challenge of fitting the proficiencies listed into a specific and limited time frame. A state website that lists pages and pages of required kindergarten proficiencies with no sense of a connecting narrative is simply a list. And teachers will hardly examine in depth a five-week-long 6th grade math module that runs more than 500 pages.

We learned one important format point in curriculum templates when we were in Finland. Many, if not most, comprehensive school programs there have students in long-term groupings with a team of three teachers over several years, providing continuity and community. Thus, they have a *three-year* curricular layout, not a year-to-year layout. There are fewer gaps because students pick up where they left off after their summer break, whereas in grade-level bands with a new teacher every year, it takes at least a month for teachers to get to know their students. Consider the following questions:

- To what extent can you loop with students, especially in preK–8? Such options deepen connections with content—and with students.
- To what extent have you prioritized key standards both horizontally and vertically? Instead of teachers cherry-picking what to focus on, faced with an untenable curriculum guide, they could work together vertically to streamline their curriculum to ensure coherence and viability across grade levels.

What an Individual Educator *Can* Control

Many curriculum designers are resigned that there is not much they can do to impact systems-level streamlining. It is depressing to take precious professional meeting time to "fill out forms" in accordance with standards when there is limited faith that it will do anything to slow the frenetic pace of content coverage.

But individual educators can offer suggestions. When clarifying problems with unit and lesson templates, consider framing some possible alternatives or some guiding questions to help generate more viable and useable expectations. Regardless of the expertise of the educator, there is immense value in having a blueprint or composition to work from. There also is real merit to "weeding your collection," as library-media specialists often do, to consider how to deepen the level of inquiry and creation students are engaging in as part of your regular practice.

In Our Next Episode . . .

It's tempting to dive directly into curriculum content for the purpose of streamlining it, yet if we do that, we're likely to miss the mark. The next episode will guide you to make content decisions that have integrity and power; these decisions are based on who your learners are and what they will need now and in the future. We clarify how important it is to base content choices on vibrant and powerful pedagogy that supports contemporary learner roles.

Episode 2

Using Modern Learner Roles to Streamline the Curriculum

Learning Target	Engage	Examine	Act
We can leverage modern learner roles to streamline curriculum narratives and corresponding assessments.	Consider how modern learner roles affect streamlining choices, curriculum narratives, and assessment designs.	Review case studies of mission statements converted into learner roles, as well as their effect on the learner's experience.	Draft learner roles based on mission and vision to focus curriculum narratives and assessment designs.

ENGAGE

Imagine walking into a learning space and being immediately struck by the productive hum, rhythm, and vitality of the participants in the room. Learners clustered around a table intensely debate an idea and how to improve on it. In another space, chill music emanates from portable speakers. Across the hall, learners are sitting in low cushioned chairs or sprawled on the floor, immersed in their individual reading or viewing experiences. Downstairs, a learner examines work with a peer coach to evaluate their current performance and strategize next steps. The participants inhabit the space and treat one another with a level of autonomy and trust. Students are *self-navigators, discerning researchers,* and *collaborative citizens.*

Step back and consider your connection to this imagined walk through. Who typically has access to a learning environment like this? Is this only possible in certain subject areas or grade levels? In only enrichment classes or private schools? Or could this represent learning experiences that might take place in both a kindergarten and a physics classroom, in both a capstone project and an internship? In such vibrant school environments, the desired outcomes for students respond to the time in which they live and the future they will inherit.

These environments don't happen in a vacuum. They're derived from a mission that matters and from pedagogy that develops modern learners. This notion of the power of mission is true in all organizations. As Khadem and Khadem (2017) point out,

> Most companies have mission, vision, and value statements as part of their business plans. They refer to them from time to time and might use them to motivate the employees, investors, suppliers, or customers. Many display them on the corridor walls or post them by the entrance to their building or on their websites. But few companies place their mission and vision at the center of everything they do, linking all their metrics to mission and vision. For alignment to happen in an organization, this is essential. Mission, vision, and core values have to be front and center. (p. 17)

Most schools have mission and vision statements, but these often have little effect on learning choices. Perhaps the statements are antiquated. Perhaps they're clear but seldom acted on. Perhaps the statements are akin to the kitchen sink—lots of ideas are thrown in, but they need streamlining.

We contend that when schools translate their missions into *actual roles for students to cultivate,* it shifts the focus of learning, the teaching approaches, and the resulting assessments throughout the system. Clarifying these active roles is the ultimate North Star. For example, in *Bold Moves for Schools,* Heidi and her coauthor, Marie Alcock, imagined a refreshed job description for both teacher and student, incorporating such roles as *self-navigator, media critic, global and local ambassador,* and *innovative designer* (Jacobs & Alcock, 2017). This second episode focuses on clarifying modern learner roles and on how these roles will influence curriculum narrative choices.

Modern Learner Roles and Curriculum Choices

Schools are interactive systems with a complex, overwhelming, and sometimes contradictory set of priorities concerning what's most important for students to learn. We contend that what's most important is supporting the aspirations of modern learners and the various learning roles they take on. That necessitates shifting to a pedagogical approach in which students are partners in their learning. It's an approach that is constructivist and inquiry based. Students have agency in what they learn, how they learn, who they're learning with, and how they're demonstrating learning. In later episodes, we will delve more deeply into this student-facing approach, considering what curriculum narratives look like, the elements you need to develop a compelling storyline, and how to lay out a storyboard written for students.

Elevating modern learner roles at the onset of the design helps us determine the learning experiences students will encounter. For example, if we hope to develop students as *social entrepreneurs,* then content choices will not just "be about" other places in the world; rather, students will actively investigate as decision makers who seek information to broaden perspectives and make meaningful improvements to their community. In response to developing the social entrepreneur role, learning experiences will provide background on specific locations and offer opportunities for connecting with others.

Consider, as an example, how shopping malls in many towns and cities are shuttering because of changes in consumer behavior. Working in the role of social entrepreneur, students could connect with businesses in a struggling mall or surrounding a newly closed mall to document the impact the mall has had on these businesses, both anecdotally and to the bottom line. Another approach might be investigating how malls have been reinvented by developers seeking "to create thriving communities that resemble town centers and feature cultural assets like schools, libraries, fitness centers, and medical clinics in addition to retail and entertainment options" (Plenge & Pilgreen, 2023, para. 2) and connect with people who have repurposed other kinds of abandoned spaces. This authentic inquiry might be folded into economics, business, marketing, civics, leadership, public speaking or entrepreneurial courses. It could also be an interdisciplinary experience connecting several courses together or the basis of an individual capstone project, job shadowing experience, or independent study. We learn about real people in real places.

Figure 2.1 illustrates how meta-level roles and pedagogy can directly inform design choices. Looking at the graphic, note that modern learner roles are devised and shaped from multiple sources:

FIGURE 2.1

Modern Learner Roles and Curricular Choices

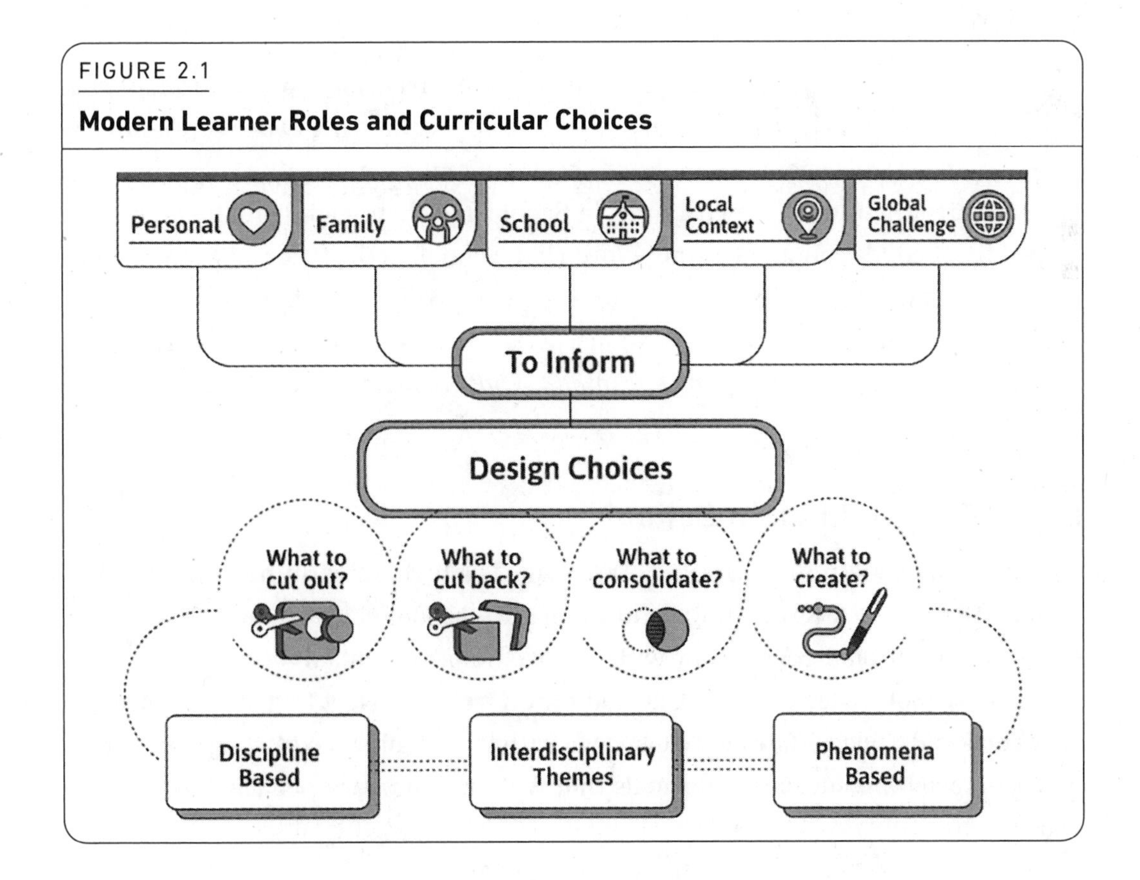

- Personal input from individuals in the school community.
- Family representation to reflect the needs of every learner.
- School input from professional staff and leadership.
- Local context reflecting the needs of the surrounding community.
- Global challenges that students should be prepared to face in the future.

When a teacher focuses squarely on developing a specific learner role, it also directly affects assessment design. Consider how a coach develops a basketball player. The focus is on the learner *as a player*. It's inherently personalized. The power of that role ripples through the streamlining process and helps the coach make choices about what matters most and how to engage the learner in the process. To play basketball, an individual needs a set of basic skills and know-how. We will explore the connection to assessment design in Episode 7.

EXAMINE

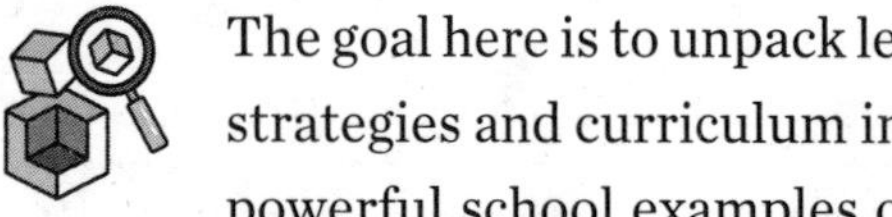

The goal here is to unpack learner roles and translate them into actionable strategies and curriculum imperatives. The following two case studies are powerful school examples of developing modern learning roles. We both had the privilege of working with Lincoln School and their leadership team. Allison helped the second school, Incarnate Word High School, in the fields of science, technology, religion, engineering, arts, and mathematics (STREAM). As you read the case studies, consider the following questions: *What language are you drawn to? What internal dialogue is happening in your mind? What connections and comparisons are you making?*

Case Study 1: Lincoln School

Lincoln School in Buenos Aires, Argentina, is a high-performing junior kindergarten through 12 (JK–12) international private school that balances the official Argentinian national curriculum with International Baccalaureate requirements. Lincoln's school leaders are using accreditation from the New England Association of Schools and Colleges (NEASC) to engage with their staff in developing a definition of learning and broader learning goals that will drive modern pedagogical practice and design.

The school's website (see www.lincoln.edu.ar/learning) defines learning as "the intentional process of making sense of the world through exploration, expression, and reflection. The journey of lifelong learning is transformative, inspires action, and opens new pathways" (para. 7). The website also highlights the four Attributes of a Lincoln Learner: the learner as thinker and researcher, the learner as change agent, the learner as communicator, and the learner as self-navigator. These broader categories include a list of roles that the school deems essential for modern learners to take on. Let's look at them now.

The learner as thinker and researcher

- The **inquirer** asks questions to explore a topic or an issue, using prior knowledge, personal experience, and cultural frames of reference.
- The **discerning problem solver** determines the roots of a problem to address its complexity and shapes a solution path.
- The **innovative designer** crafts imaginative and purposeful solutions, findings, prototypes, performances, and media using design thinking and inquiry processes.
- The **critical researcher** analyzes a range of data sources and viewpoints while ethically using the research process.

The learner as change agent

- The **global and local ambassador** engages with others to explore contemporary issues in local and global contexts and proposes solutions that will improve the lives of others.
- The **ethical citizen** makes ethical choices and demonstrates integrity by anticipating and evaluating the consequences of words and actions in view of promoting positive results in the community.
- The **advocate for justice, equity, diversity, and inclusion (JEDI)** embraces diversity and advocates for inclusive practices that promote equity and justice.

The learner as communicator

- The **responsive listener** contributes to interactions by respectfully seeking to better understand someone's point of view, using home or acquired languages.

- The **critical reader** works to comprehend and analyze different texts, in home or acquired languages, across various disciplines for multiple purposes.
- The **articulate speaker** expresses information and ideas, being mindful of purpose and audience in home or acquired languages.
- The **effective writer** generates rich and well-crafted texts that show a command of language and are informed by the use of genre and evidence in home or acquired languages.
- The **creative producer** expresses complex ideas creatively, in home or acquired languages, by producing original work that emulates professional techniques using a range of contemporary media formats.

The learner as self-navigator

- The **self-monitor** cultivates a growth mindset toward understanding their own emotions, thoughts, and behavior and develops interests and pursues goals with purpose and efficacy.
- The **self-manager** prepares for learning; plans for timelines and the completion of work; manages their own emotions, thoughts, and behaviors; and contributes positively to school culture and climate.
- The **relationship-builder** establishes, maintains, and advocates for healthy and supportive relationships with culturally diverse individuals and groups and collaborates with empathy. They work effectively in teams while resisting negative social pressure, resolving conflicts constructively and seeking or offering help when needed.

Examining Lincoln's process can help school leaders guide this work in their own schools. To begin with, the leaders drafted learning goals—their Attributes of a Lincoln Learner (ALLs)—that reflected a vision of what's possible rather than simply being an audit of what *is*. They shared these learning goals with faculty for their feedback and then publicly shared them on their school website for prospective families and staff to review. The ALLs are now an impetus for action in the planning of curriculum, lessons, and assessments.

As you reflect on this work, consider the following:

- How might you involve teachers in drafting these seminal documents?
- What role might students and their families play in the design of these aims?

- What type of learning experiences might be part of these students' typical assessment and instructional practices?
- What pedagogical practices come to mind that align with the ALLs?

Case Study 2: Incarnate Word High School

Incarnate Word High School in San Antonio, Texas (see www.incarnatewordhs.org), is a private Catholic all-girls school committed to developing the next generation of women leaders. The principal introduced the school to Allison as a "140+–year startup"; the founding sisters were entrepreneurial in envisioning and building a school committed to Christian service and leadership. The learner goals were first generated by focus groups of students, staff, parents, alumni, and women professionals who were speaking at one of the school's STREAM events. Approximately 10 percent of students were involved in generating and refining the following roles:

- The **global leader** seeks out and pursues challenges with an open mind to guide investigations, solutions, and actions in service to greater well-being for others and stewardship in keeping with the seven themes of Catholic social teaching.
- The **strategic thinker** examines and critiques information from diverse sources to reach an evidence-based conclusion or solution.
- The **faith-based community member** celebrates God's presence through prayer, sacrifice, service, and moral living to serve others with compassion and empathy.
- The **self-directed learner** initiates a plan of action, prioritizes tasks, manages time, monitors progress, and seeks support as needed to develop and demonstrate their God-given potential.
- The **creative thinker and innovator** demonstrates original, imaginative, and innovative ways of thinking to develop new and meaningful ideas, solutions, or ventures.
- The **open-minded inquirer** generates compelling questions and seeks answers through research, reason, and reflection.
- The **effective communicator** develops and clarifies ideas when speaking, writing, or creating, based on a given purpose and target audience.
- The **self-aware learner** actively reflects on productive struggle to better understand individual motivations and needs in order to refine

boundaries, ask for support, and become a more confident and humbler God-centered woman.

- The **empowered digital learner** uses technology in productive and responsible ways to adapt, create, consume, and connect in social, academic, and professional settings.
- The **trusted collaborator** contributes to and works effectively in teams by respecting diverse viewpoints, being open to what others are thinking and feeling, displaying compassion, developing consensus, and taking action on feedback to achieve a shared goal.

Entrusting students to partner in the design and development of their learning is both powerful and rare. The focus group members, including the young women, received updates on the strategic vision of the school, with key areas of focus being to increase dual-credit course offerings with higher education partners and develop STREAM offerings (a guest speaker program as well as place-based experiences). They are becoming oriented to these learner roles through their self-directed capstone projects and co-curricular learning opportunities. The STREAM leadership team and school alumni are connecting with local and global partners to launch and sustain opportunities aligned to the learning goals. Teaching staff are reexamining and revising assessments to integrate these learner roles into their coursework.

ACT

Modern learner roles are overarching, transdisciplinary, and lifelong. Educators can use them in a myriad of ways, such as to reexamine dated scope and sequences, revisit one-size-fits-all policies, and generate new learning opportunities aligned to place-based learning experiences. The following suggestions may be valuable in guiding this work.

How to Develop Criteria

We propose the following key criteria for developing modern learner roles:

- Select a reasonable number of goals. These should cover a range of skills, behaviors, and dispositions. Limiting these to 10 may be helpful.

- Ensure that goals encompass topics and challenges that learners encounter in all dimensions of school life—in their curricular, social, and personal investigations. These will lend themselves to both transdisciplinary and subject-specific tasks that honor existing curricular choices, as well as expand design opportunities to more meaningfully include students.
- Ensure that goals have depth and breadth, that they're both complex and sophisticated. The goals can be broken down into subskills and grade-level bands for instruction and coaching.
- Provide clarity and specifics. Avoid broad generalizations. Fuzzy language implies fuzzy thinking.

How to Gather Information

Engaging with families, community members, and students on shared aspirations helps clarify priorities and strengthens relationships. Certainly, formal planning meetings, traditional surveys, and interviews can be helpful, but we particularly appreciate "listening tours" that can be conducted both virtually or on site. Whether it's a morning coffee at school, an evening Zoom meeting, or an afternoon discussion session, reaching out to busy parents in more relaxed settings can be highly effective. Inviting key stakeholders to be part of the design process builds understanding about modern learner roles and how to use them.

How to Generate New Learning Roles

Many schools often focus on the management of a task rather than on the relationships needed to successfully complete that task. For example, being a *productive and thoughtful collaborator* is a dynamic between the way people interact and the work they need to accomplish. Future forward learning goals value both. Here's our initial draft of one such goal:

> Cultivates relationships with all members of the school community to build on, better understand, and actively engage with one another's perspectives.
>
> - Through listening and questioning, communicates with others in increasingly skillful ways to develop more effective thinking.
> - Recognizes how positive relationships affect motivation, openness to new ideas, and connection to the work.

- Adheres to norms and demonstrates respectful behaviors to foster a safe environment that invites all to participate.

Too often, we identify powerful roles, but we simply do a drive-by with them. Take the term *critical thinkers,* for example. We may assume that everyone already knows what the role means or that it's already incorporated into classroom pedagogy and practices. Inventure Academy in Bangalore, India, a school with which Allison is currently working, has taken a more proactive stance. Because growing critical thinkers is one of the modern learner roles in their mission, the school team first delineated the essential thinking dispositions they wanted to develop in their students: self-awareness, inquiry, analysis and critique, collaborative knowledge construction, and openness to new ideas. They then articulated a learner progression to help teachers frame curriculum, assessment, and instructional choices in student-facing language.

Figure 2.2 shows a portion of that learner progression, highlighting two facets of critical thinkers: self-awareness and inquiry. The progression defines the facets and then describes them in terms of four levels of mastery.

At the close of the session in which they did this work, many staff members at Inventure Academy said they were moved by the depth and complexity of a term they had previously thought they understood. They were excited about the possibilities of homing in on the facets of critical thinking with their students. The school will prototype the complete learner progression with students to ensure its clarity and accessibility so they can use the tool to gauge where students are and monitor their growth.

Moving Beyond Wall Art

When schools adopt meta-level goals, they often end up as wall art—enshrined on posters and web pages, with a limited effect on curriculum and instructional choices. Here's what it looks like when goals do—and don't—inform curriculum choices:

- When goals *do* inform curriculum choices, **teachers** identify, create, and redesign compelling problems, questions, and challenges that refresh the curriculum storyline. When they *don't,* we're more likely to recycle what we have in front of us, cover old material, and miss an opportunity.

FIGURE 2.2

Two Facets of Critical Thinkers, with Four Levels of Development

Facets of Critical Thinkers	Level 1	Level 2	Level 3	Level 4
Self-Awareness *I can apply metacognitive and reflective thinking to better understand the topic and learn more about my own thinking.*	I am beginning to become more aware of how and what I am thinking about this topic.	I am aware of perspectives and opinions other than my own and consider how they might influence my thinking.	I am increasingly aware of how a perspective or an opinion is based on prior knowledge, personal experience, and implicit bias.	I show a willingness to change or deepen my perspective or opinion through regular examination and reflection.
Inquiry *I can develop and refine questions to guide my investigation or analysis.*	I develop questions to build basic comprehension about a topic, text, or problem.	I develop a range of questions and select one or two that interest me to guide my investigation, analysis, or approach.	I expand my thinking as I investigate key questions I have chosen. I develop and refine my questions, taking into consideration multiple perspectives.	I elaborate on and extend my thinking on the basis of tentative answers to my questions. I persist in questioning as I seek more information and consider further areas of inquiry.

Source: Inventure Academy, Bangalore, India. Used with permission.

- When goals *do* inform curriculum choices, **students** become more skillful, sophisticated, and strategic throughout their school years. When they *don't,* students are savvy enough to see that what matters most to teachers and to their parents doesn't align with the modern learner roles posted on the wall.
- When goals *do* inform curriculum choices, the **school community** reaches consensus on realistic priorities that are central to the school's efforts and that guide decision making. When they *don't,* the school community may resort to the granular, falling back on priorities, such as rote memorization, that are no longer relevant to the modern learner. (See Jacobs & Zmuda, n.d.)

In Our Next Episode . . .

Now that we know which modern learner roles we need to cultivate, the next step is to begin streamlining curriculum content. However, this doesn't mean simply paring down content; that would just perpetuate an antiquated curriculum. In Episode 3, we'll look at using the broader aims of schooling to guide our streamlining efforts and develop a refreshed storyline. What do we cut? Consolidate? Create?

Episode 3

What to Cut Out, Cut Back, Consolidate, and Create

Learning Target	Engage	Examine	Act
We can streamline our curriculum by making thoughtful choices about what it contains.	Explore how the editorial stance leads to effective curriculum streamlining.	Analyze examples from schools that have streamlined curriculum in three ways: in a disciplinary, an interdisciplinary, and a phenomena-based setting.	Make choices about what to cut out, cut back, consolidate, and create at a system or classroom level.

ENGAGE

Given that *curriculum* literally means "a path to run in small steps," it's important to engage learners in seeing the narrative arc in their learning experiences. For example, the "story" of math must address the following questions: *How do all the concepts, standards, and proficiencies we are learning this year connect with one another? How do they connect to the math concepts, standards, and proficiencies we learned last year, learned in the years prior, and will learn through senior year?* If these connections aren't clear to the teacher, then finding them will be even more daunting for learners. Algebra students should be able to tell the "story" of how to imagine, model, and represent problems in different but equivalent ways; those who cannot provide that narrative flow will likely be adrift when encountering geometry.

An Editor's Stance

As curriculum designers, teachers may play varied and interconnected roles—as *researchers* to explore and identify problems, challenges, and resources; as *developers* to identify or generate assignments; or as *initial users* to test out unit prototypes. But too often the role of *editor* is relegated to more trivial matters, such as making sure all the boxes are filled in correctly. According to one definition (Definitions.net, n.d.), "An editor's role is the art, technique, and practice of assembling individual moments into a coherent sequence." For example, "a film editor must creatively work with the layers of images, story, dialogue, music, pacing, as well as the actors' performances to effectively 're-imagine' and even rewrite the film to craft a cohesive whole."

A fundamental part of the editor's role is using a wide-angle lens to look for a narrative arc that reveals a storyline. When we tell stories, we make sense of our lives to communicate what we experience, see, and learn. Here in Episode 3, we show how to make that curriculum narrative possible by streamlining content, resources, and standards.

How to Streamline

Making informed choices in this area requires an editorial eye both at the system and classroom levels. It may be helpful to refer to the visual shown in Figure 2.1 (see p. 27) to frame curriculum choices.

- **What to cut out.** Teachers can make proactive and deliberate choices to remove whole topics, units, novels, or projects. Eliminate the unnecessary by considering what matters most for students when they encounter a curriculum. By reviewing the work at previous grade levels, teachers can better determine which material might be redundant.
- **What to cut back.** Teachers can cut back on interesting but unnecessary tangents, topics that subsequent grade levels will more meaningfully address, and redundant resources and assignments.
- **What to consolidate.** Teachers can identify connections among units and then combine those units. The point is integration. As teachers consider the layout of the academic year, they can look for intersections where concepts overlap. Interdisciplinary possibilities often emerge when consolidating.
- **What to create.** Teachers can develop new topics to support the curriculum narrative. They can include diverse perspectives that honor the lived experiences of their communities. They can offer space for learners to more deeply investigate, create, and revise, as well as space for teachers to provide just-in-time teaching, regular feedback, and personalized tasks.

Although most teachers would agree that their current curriculum is overrun with too many activities, resources, and topics, the icon of the scissors later in this episode (see p. 49) may cause them some concern. Who gives them "permission" to cut out or cut back material? How might that affect their colleagues, whether in their grade level, course, or vertically, in making sure students are prepared for more challenging topics?

Snipping Away at the Standards

Cutting back or cutting out standards is an immediate concern, especially if you were to do it haphazardly or unintentionally. We suggest examining standards documents to identify core categories or bundles. When laying them out in what our colleague Marie Alcock calls a yearlong context, you can bundle the standards across the year as a narrative. *They are the story of the year in standards* that will naturally interface with the planned unit of study.

Here's an example. As a 3rd grade teacher lays out her units of study in language arts across the academic year, she might start with a four-week unit on What Makes a Good Story, bundling targeted Common Core standards from RL (reading literature), W (writing standards related to responding to stories), and SL (speaking and listening that focus on narrative). That unit would be followed by a five-week unit on Investigating Topics, in which the teacher bundles standards from RI (reading informational text), standards in writing (W) focused on gathering and analyzing information, and corresponding SL (speaking and listening) standards.

Working with bundled standards saves teachers hours of planning and cross-checking long lists of categories. But what's even more powerful is translating these bundles into student-facing learning targets—that is, into "I can" statements. Take a look at how the 3rd grade teacher might translate one of her reading standards into two accessible parts, both of which could be the basis for lessons and engagement assessments.

> **RL.3.3:** Describe characters in a story (e.g., their traits, motivations, or feelings) and explain how their actions contribute to the sequence of events.
>
> **Learning Targets:** "I can describe the traits of the characters" and "I can explain how the character affected what happened in the story."

If teachers received easy-to-use bundled standards that were converted into learning targets, they could get straight to the work of planning rather than spending hours translating the work into practice.

Unearthing possible storylines will clarify what is still vital in the curriculum and what is no longer necessary. But take note: cutting back or cutting out may also threaten learning designs that teachers have perfected over the years. This gut-wrenching weeding of what is familiar, what a teacher may take tremendous pride in even though it may no longer have value, may generate resentment or grief.

EXAMINE

As we begin to take an editorial stance, it's helpful to illustrate how other schools have done it. The first is a *discipline-based* example from a high school where the goal was to streamline each course within a given subject area, which we follow with an *interdisciplinary* example in an elementary school. Finally, we offer several *phenomena-based* examples to spark interest in those possibilities. All three curriculum settings will get a closer look in Episode 5.

Editing the Curriculum: A Discipline-Based Example

Cutting out, cutting back, and consolidating may feel impossible to do—especially if you start with the first unit in a course at the beginning of the year and attempt to make modest modifications throughout. The trick is to examine the standards to unearth concepts that are worthy of being the basis for a curriculum narrative. And it helps to be clear about what *worthy* means. You want to be able to answer "yes" to the following questions:

- Is the concept directly aligned to priority standards?
- Does it offer students authentic opportunities to do or experience something?
- Does it reveal the power of this discipline—for example, math (or poetry or music) as a powerful and elegant language to describe the world?
- Does it connect to the broader aspirations we have for our students?
- Will the concept energize our students to immerse themselves more deeply in the course content?

Figure 3.1 shows how to approach course content when the world is your oyster—that is, when you're teaching 9th grade world history. Social studies teachers could step back and identify key learner roles they want to develop: modern-day historians, investigative researchers, and media makers. They could then identify a narrative approach that is a connective thread as they explore the world rather than an eclectic and disconnected journey.

Editing the Curriculum: An Interdisciplinary Example

Our second example comes from Connecticut's New Haven Public School Magnet Division, where Heidi has had the opportunity to work for more than five years. Under the auspices of a federal grant, identified schools each take on a theme to use as a "North Star." The theme chosen was "Community Connectors: East Rock, New Haven, and the World." Each grade-level team from kindergarten through 8th grade developed three rigorous interdisciplinary curriculum experiences around three topics, issues, or problems that link back to the theme; in the units that resulted, students developed projects, connected directly with the community, and used their

FIGURE 3.1

A 9th Grade World History Course: A Disciplinary Approach

What to cut out? *Make room for deeper investigation and development of key concepts and skills.*	**What to cut back?** *Foreground important cognitive and technical skills, content that is central to the big idea, and commitment to demonstrations of learning that are most revealing and helpful.*	**What to consolidate?** *Combine elements to make a more effective coherent whole.*	**What to create?** *Provide a fresh perspective for learners bringing multiple subject areas on common topics, problems, issues, and themes.*
Eliminate unnecessary names and dates. Within each unit identify the "highlight" reel and cut out tangents.	Reduce exit ticket quizzes. Reduce the number of compelling questions to only the most essential. Shift from basing daily tasks on the textbook to using the textbook as a story spine.	Pull together related events within the unit and between units throughout the year. Avoid isolated events and key historical figures. Integrate readings.	Be historians! Gather historical artifacts. Share using modern media for documentary making. View more media with readings. Create a digital interactive timeline for the year.

creativity. The curriculum was scaffolded vertically and aligned to the Connecticut State Standards.

Figure 3.2 shows the kindergarten sequence for the year. As you can see, the first unit focused on the question "How can I help my school community be a happier place?" As teachers developed the curriculum for this theme, they continually reflected on what to cut out, cut back, consolidate, and create.

Editing the Curriculum: Phenomena-Based Examples

This last set of scenarios is perhaps the most rewarding: exploring issues, events, settings, situations, and discoveries that are current and relevant to the learner but not preplanned in the curriculum. These moments are all around us; they arise in the

FIGURE 3.2

A Kindergarten Sequence: An Interdisciplinary Approach

Grade Level	Unit 1	Unit 2	Unit 3
Kinder-garten	**Piecing Together East Rock** *How can I help my school community be a happier place?* Our kindergartners will be reporters and will interview teachers, administrators, staff members, and students throughout the building. Teachers and children will co-create interview questions to ask throughout the process, including inquiring into the important roles of the people in our town of East Rock. We will create an "East Rock puzzle" composed of pictures of the students, as well as of people they have interviewed outside class. 	**New Haven Helps Us Read** *How do people in our community help me with my reading?* *How do we use reading, writing, speaking, and listening in our everyday life?* Kindergarten students will explore the important roles that individuals and organizations play in helping them become readers. We will visit the public library, the Yale Bookstore, and the organization New Haven Reads, and we will learn about the ways they support our readers. Together we will hold an East Rock Community and Cultural Magnet School book drive. We will seek donations from students and families. We will also invite staff to come and read to our students. Each student will have an older student reading buddy. 	**A Slice of New Haven** *What makes New Haven's pizzeria history unique?* New Haven is famous for its delicious pizza. East Rock's kindergarten classes will focus on the extensive history of New Haven pizza. We will take field trips to different pizzerias in the city to interview and interact with owners of and workers in these establishments. We will create a timeline of select New Haven pizzerias, specifically ones that we are able to visit or contact directly. We will include facts, photos, menus, and reviews of their pizza. In one-minute commercials, we will promote New Haven pizzerias. 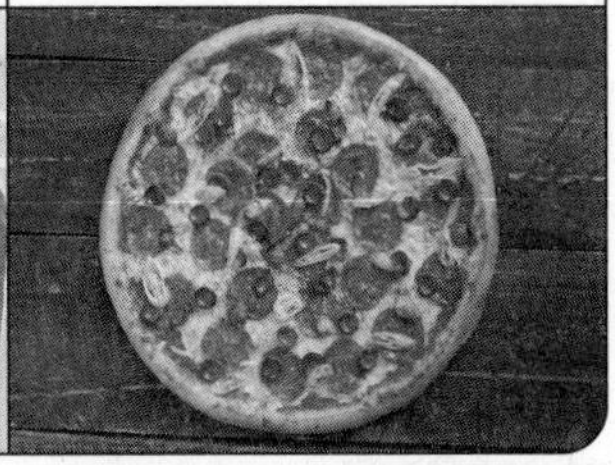

Source: East Rock Community and Cultural Studies Magnet School, New Haven, Connecticut. Used with permission.

lives of our students and the larger world in which they live. And they give authentic opportunities to apply thinking dispositions. For example, teachers at a Brooklyn preschool listened to the talk about the moon, stars, and planets (Saturn in particular) generated by 4-year-olds at the play tables, on the monkey bars, and in circle time. The children couldn't get enough of the images from space and requested stories about them. Following the lead of the learners, the teachers launched an investigation of the name and image of each planet, the order of the planets from closest to farthest from the sun, and a unique quality about each planet. The enormous red spot on Jupiter and Saturn's rings were both big hits.

Serendipity is at play when a student is motivated by a personal and an immediate experience or when a group of students is affected by an event on the local or global stage. Pursuing that natural thread of conversation and interest is precisely what phenomena-based learning espouses. It prepares students to live more fully, and it raises their awareness of what matters most.

Many schools prefer a more stable format to anchor the experience. The four options that follow may already be a feature in your school, but we have paired them with a reimagined version of what each could look like. What appears first is a typical example of an isolated event in a student's schedule: current events, genius hour, capstone projects, and the United Nations Sustainable Goals. Given the isolated nature of these offerings, students may not delve into what's fascinating in the topic because they feel it's tangential to the game of school. Conversely, when they go back to their regularly scheduled programming, they may often become more insistent for the teachers to explain "why this should matter to me." The reimagined version makes phenomena-based learning more than a token gesture.

Current events

What They Are: This is a block of time during the day when teachers and students share news items that pique their interest. To provide focus, teachers may provide a designated theme or topic for students to look for. Current events can be a more formal expectation with a summative grade or can remain an informal and ungraded experience.

What They Could Be: Curriculum editors could design an expectation where students periodically review the collection of current events they have discussed so far to identify one that interests them. The students would then research that topic to find additional resources to promote deeper understanding. If the current events are restricted to the subject or course focus, teachers can develop a curriculum project pairing the *emergent topics* that students find fascinating with preplanned expectations, such as time allotted, instructional scaffolds, and rubrics.

Genius hour

What It Is: This is a once-a-week block of time where students explore a topic that fascinates them. Students may network with others for feedback, consider how to "end" the project to exhibit learning, and explore ways to evaluate their work that focuses on idea generation and process. Topics may connect to their long-term, Future Forward Learning Goals.

What It Could Be: Curriculum editors could leverage student-generated questions to inspire revised curriculum topics and reimagined projects. For example, a student may use their genius hour time to learn more about the internationally reported discovery in 2021 that there used to be water on Mars, which then was replaced with evidence in 2022 that water in the form of ice exists on Mars today. Their questions? What does ice on Mars portend for future exploration on Mars? What does it suggest about the history of life on the planet? This personal, unfettered exploration can influence explorations in Earth and space science or can serve as a high-interest topic to grow discerning readers in English language arts. Curriculum editors could include students at the curriculum design table by asking them what questions they uncovered, what resources were most helpful, and what ideas were most intriguing during their exploration. The goal of genius hour was always to spark ideas and grow curiosity through investigation and idea development. With this reimagining, it can spread back and revitalize other disciplines.

Passion or capstone projects

What They Are: These are typically 3- to 12-month-long investigations where students explore a topic of interest, with a clear expectation of a formal evaluation at the end of it. Because this is a special event, rare in their learning experience, students may struggle to come up with something compelling to research and may treat this opportunity as just one more hurdle on their way to graduation.

What They Could Be: Most existing parameters of passion or capstone projects are clear about the intent: students design a compelling question or idea, immerse themselves in the investigation, and develop an artifact that illustrates what they've learned about the topic and themselves along the way. If students are offered more time *throughout the school day* to explore such issues, they will be more fully engaged in such projects because they'll see them as a natural extension of their learning rather than as an isolated event.

United Nations Sustainable Development Goals

What They Are: The Sustainable Development Goals (SDGs) were developed by the United Nations to inspire global innovation and action by 2030 (United Nations Development Programme [UNDP], n.d.), and they're often the basis of a project in social studies or science classrooms. Sustainable cities, clean water and sanitation, and affordable and clean energy continue to be emergent topics that are aligned to science standards. Curriculum editors may already be using the SDGs in their subject-area classrooms to inspire students to study local, national, and global problems and design, prototype, and share proposed solutions.

What They Could Be: When the United Nations member states first adopted the SDGs in 2015, the developers clarified the integration among the goals in this way: "Action in one area will affect outcomes in others, and that development must balance social, economic, and environmental sustainability" (UNDP, n.d., para. 2). Curriculum editors can consider how to benefit from this integration and how it might inspire interdisciplinary approaches as students immerse themselves in these emergent issues.

For example, in New Jersey's West Windsor–Plainsboro school district, each of the district's 800 8th graders are involved in a week-long interdisciplinary project that engages them in tackling one of the SDGs. For example, the first goal deals with ending poverty; the second, with ending hunger; and the third, with ensuring good health and well-being. Students must research their chosen challenge, define the root problem, consider possible options, and propose a well-reasoned solution to a panel of community judges. Along the way, they collaborate with a diverse team of fellow students and communicate through a variety of media to members of the community, former and future teachers, high school students, and, for some, experts in the field of global development.

Mark Wise, a K–12 curriculum supervisor for the district and a Global Challenge Project leader whose work is based on the SDGs, has noted the district's continued commitment *across the school year* to building student capacity to meet their district mission. (See Zmuda, n.d., for a guest post from Wise on this topic.) If students are only afforded that kind of academic freedom and authentic learning experience in an isolated school experience, it won't inform teaching and learning across the district. As a result of the school's commitment to this work, teachers are more deliberate in offering meaningful choices and learning pathways, in seeking authentic audiences for student work, and in reducing teacher over-scaffolding to give students more leeway to apply their learning to new and complex problems and open-ended scenarios.

ACT

Before we outline some actions that vertical teams or pilot groups could take, let's look at what an individual educator might do to take an editorial stance.

- **Set aside time for a close read of the standards.** Many standards are written in complex sentences with technical language that sometimes can be off-putting. We suggest getting a strong cup of coffee and breaking up the task into multiple reading sessions. Identify what each standard really requires and circle words that are unfamiliar or vague. Working with colleagues in person or online, review the supporting documentation from the state department of education, regional agency, or national organization. Identifying the scope of the standard (*think: assessment boundary in the Next Generation Science Standards*) can clarify how much territory needs to be covered and what the standardized assessments are likely to address.
- **Lay out your existing unit topics with their *real* time frame.** Even a superhero teacher cannot meaningfully cover everything. On a virtual card or sticky note, write the title of each unit and the amount of time it actually takes rather than what's listed in the pacing guide. Then, reflect on and respond to this question: *If students really "got the point" of this unit, what will they be better equipped to do or make sense of with increased independence?*
- **Play with the unit order.** Could you move some of the units around to build a pattern or narrative thread? Considering the various possibilities can give you fresh ideas about how to consolidate and cut back.
- **Ask students what they find to be compelling.** Engage students in monthly or quarterly conversations around your course content. W*hat do they wish they could do more of or less of? What did they find intriguing? What did they wish they had more time to explore or create?*

- **Be transparent.** When exploring how to make the curriculum documents more usable (e.g., *realistic, compelling to students,* and *with a deeper connection to modern learner roles*), doing so in a vacuum may alienate colleagues and supervisors. Taking an editorial eye to your work to hone and expand practices is a necessity, but it also can be disruptive when fresh thinking affects uninformed colleagues.

The scale of the review process in terms of curriculum streamlining depends on how invested a school is in systemic curriculum planning. Figure 3.3 lists the criteria for a review, as well as actions you might take. There could be a formal review of K–12 or a departmental or across-grade-level review. In a school with limited systemic curriculum mapping, the review clearly falls on individual teachers, who will need to streamline their own curriculum across a school year.

Begin by developing a powerful set of learner aspirations or school mission statements that we call *future forward learning goals*. These might include such goals as *focus on developing inquiry to better understand complex issues* or *focus on listening with understanding and empathy*. Then use the following five-step process to examine existing curriculum in any of the three approaches we described—disciplinary, interdisciplinary, or phenomena based—to determine what matters most for your learners. Although this weeding may be painful for some, it will relieve pressure for coverage and provide more space to generate new ideas with students (see Jacobs & Zmuda, n.d.).

Step 1: Identify the area needing review in your curriculum.

Whether it's disciplinary, interdisciplinary, or phenomena based, identify the course, grade level, or grade-level bands in need of review. Compile existing units of study in that course or curriculum area.

Step 2: Determine who should be on the review team.

Consider points of view that will provide fresh perspectives. The number of members on a team is proportional to school size. Some options are preexisting groups, such as department chairs or curriculum councils, and ad hoc groups, such as vertical teams or interdisciplinary teams. Select people who will add value to the review.

FIGURE 3.3

How to Streamline Your Curriculum

Editorial Focus	Establish Criteria for Review	Conduct Review and Generate Possible Actions
Make room for deeper investigation and development of key concepts and skills.	Make cuts to highlight what matters most, given time constraints and the specific learners, and decide what to let go. • Situation conditions—such as a shortened academic calendar, staggered classroom schedules, alternative onsite attendance, and increased online learning demand—will influence decisions.	When making decisions about cutting a unit, identify crucial standards and foreground them when designing learning experiences. • Bundling standards that naturally cluster together helps distinguish standards that are crucial from those that are not.
Foreground important cognitive and technical skills, content that is central to the big idea, and key demonstrations of learning.	Review the thumbnail story of the curriculum through the year to determine the placement of units. • Cut back by distinguishing most crucial elements from less crucial elements. • Consider cuts in skills, content, and assessments as you determine criteria.	Determining skill, content, and assessment cuts requires setting clear priorities about what is essential for learners. • **Skills:** Elevate skills that are integral to a given discipline, as well as subskills tied to Future Forward Learning Goals. • **Content:** Confront the tendency to cover content. —Distinguish content that directly supports and is central to the Future Forward Learning Goals and storyline. —Given the larger aims and goals of the unit, cut nonessential materials, information, facts, and subtopics. • **Assessment:** Evidence of learning is the bedrock of learning experience design. —Determine as a faculty which formative and summative assessments, as well as which demonstrations of learning, are the most revealing across grade levels and vertically. —If there are cuts in the curriculum, then there will be corresponding cuts in the assessments.

(continued)

FIGURE 3.3

How to Streamline Your Curriculum *(continued)*

Editorial Question	Establish Criteria for Review	Conduct Review and Generate Possible Actions
Combine elements to make a more effective coherent whole.	Search for related and clear connections within a unit or among units, then combine them when possible. • Review the scope and sequence of a year's units to see where to merge units of study.	Consolidation can occur within an existing unit by pulling together concepts or materials that overlap. • Designing interdisciplinary units of study can be fruitful when consolidating content, whether within a course or among subjects and courses.
Provide fresh perspectives for learners, bringing in multiple subject areas as lenses through which to consider common topics, problems, issues, and themes.	Relevance means generating new curriculum units or projects that are responsive to learners. • Viewing content through the lenses of multiple subject areas can provide fresh perspectives. • Consider including phenomena-based learning that supports inquiry into emergent problems and issues in students' lives. • What is key is the immediacy of the situation under consideration, whether it's personal, local, or global.	Learners can examine current and relevant topics, problems, issues, case studies, and themes either as individual units or as a series of units. • Create engaging and timely learning experiences that are personal, local, or global. • Replace a more dated unit with a fresher one. A unit might focus on a breakthrough in science, a historical research find, a new work of literature, a seasonal change in a tree on the elementary school playground, or a local issue under debate.

Step 3: Examine each unit, and tell a brief story (that is, provide a thumbnail synopsis) of that unit.

Why does the unit exist? What essential learning will students develop and transfer when that unit is over? What are the most crucial standards to include? Review the storyline through the scope of the year. Are there connections among the units? What does your curriculum value the most?

Step 4: Conduct the review process using editorial criteria.

See Figure 3.3 for the editorial prompts—what to cut out, what to cut back, what to consolidate, and what to create. Also included are coaching points on how to establish criteria for reviewing targeted curriculum areas. For example, you must consider cuts in skills, content, and assessments to focus on the unit's larger aims and goals.

Step 5: Take action on the reviews and share them with colleagues.

The purpose of the review process is to streamline curriculum in support of learner growth and engagement. As an instructional team, teachers should share the effects of this streamlining on student learning. Teachers will experience relief and excitement at the prospect of focusing time and effort on realistic and attainable goals that they have hammered out with a professional learning community. This is a tremendous opportunity to open the window and let the world in.

In Our Next Episode . . .

After an editorial review of what matters most in the curriculum, teachers can turn their focus from editorial decisions to design choices. Episode 4 will show you how the curriculum storyboard's neurofriendly format supports direct student engagement. Through it, the narrative of the curriculum emerges.

Episode 4

The Power of a Storyline

Learning Target	Engage	Examine	Act
We can compose curriculum as a narrative to engage learners in identifying meaningful connections.	Explore why curriculum framed as narrative is more memorable for students.	Model what curriculum narratives look like using two storyboard examples.	Review and reflect on current curriculum plans to generate possibilities.

ENGAGE

When we tell stories, we're communicating what we've experienced, seen, heard, and learned—usually in a way that helps us make sense of our lives. Likewise, the story of a course should be sense-making and answer the question *How do the concepts, standards, and proficiencies connect?*

Following a *curriculum narrative*—an account of connected events—helps the learner make sense of the sequence and purpose of units. For example, one narrative of learning to read might begin in the fall when a student masters consonant blends and the vowel sound "e" and end in the spring with the student proficiently reading sight words and sentences. When learners are enlisted as partners in laying out that pathway so that they know how and why they are traveling from Point A to Point Z, they become more confident emerging readers. The term *storyline* underscores the motion of a narrative carrying a reader through an unfolding plot. With a narrative approach, a middle school student in Algebra I will be about to tell the story of how their learning progresses from understanding what an equation is to learning how to balance an equation and why that is useful. A high school history student learning about the Cold War will be able to identify its beginnings in the armistice documents from World War II.

Engaging learners in interpreting the narrative thread is essential to capturing their attention, piquing their curiosity, and arousing their emotions; it facilitates connections and encourages learners to take action. In *Wired for Story* (2012), Lisa Cron asserts,

> As counterintuitive as it may sound, a story is not about the plot or even what happens in it. Stories are about how we, rather than the world around us, change. They grab us only when they allow us to experience how it would feel to navigate the plot. Thus, the story is an internal journey, not an external one. (p. 11)

The fact that narratives connect to us as human beings is underscored from a neuroscience perspective. Humans are "fundamentally emotionally driven beings; we act in response to neurochemical levels in our brains" (Holston, 2019, para. 33). A story enables a learner to grasp concepts more quickly and effectively; the emotional components attract the amygdala (the emotional center of the brain), and a familiar story structure makes sense to the hippocampus, which helps store these episodes. Neurologist, teacher, and author Judy Willis (2017) provides this clarification:

> The four-step structure of narrative—beginning (*Once upon a time*...), problem, resolution, and ending (... *and they all lived happily ever after*)—forms a mental map onto which new information can be laid.
>
> When that new information, whether from algebra or history, is presented in the familiar narrative form, the memory structure facilitates the brain's retention of that information. Weaving learning into a story makes learning more interesting, activates the brain's positive emotional state, and hooks the information into a strong memory template. The memory then becomes more durable as the learning follows the narrative pattern through sequences connected to a theme, time flow, or actions directed toward solving a problem or reaching a known goal. (paras. 9–10)

This notion of a beginning, middle, and end also mirrors the organizing narrative framework of the episodes in our book, as well as the lesson structures of learning sets.

Why Narratives Are Compelling to the Brain

The medium of storytelling often is heralded as an effective approach to engaging learners—and recent neuroscience studies reveal why. In "How Stories Connect and Persuade Us: Unleashing the Brain Power of Narrative" (Renken, 2020), the author reported that different areas of the brain light up on functional MRI scans when the subject is listening to a narrative. In that same article, Liz Neeley, the former executive director of Story Collider, notes,

> Brain networks [are] involved in deciphering—or imagining—another person's motives and the areas involved in guessing what will happen next are activated. ... Imagining what drives other people—which feeds into our predictions—helps us see a situation from different perspectives. It can even shift our core beliefs .... when we come back out of the story world into regular life. (para. 8).

Quoted in another article (McMurray, 2021), Neeley notes that stories "serve as a collective sensemaking process ... the ways in which we knit together events, that we postulate about causality, that we resolve ambiguity. We identify who the heroes are and who the villains are" (para. 11). Designing curriculum through a narrative approach can make ideas approachable, relatable, and, most important, memorable to the learner.

On the flip side, what happens when the student experiences curriculum units and classroom activities as isolated chunks of disconnected experiences? Quite simply, it diminishes the effect, and recall becomes a challenge. McTighe and Willis (2019) provide clarification:

> Rote memorization produces isolated and somewhat feeble circuits unlinked to other networks. Such shallow memories only allow learners to "give back" what was taught, mirroring the way it was taught. This limits their ability to transfer—that is, to apply their learning to new situations beyond the original context in which it was learned... Without this mental manipulation, the short-term memory fades in less than a minute. (pp. 15–16)

The current reality of curriculum pacing guides and external standards exacerbates the tension many teachers feel, whether they're teaching to the test or teaching the students in front of them. Authors Whitman and Kelleher (2016) explain the effect on students of a coverage-oriented learning experience like this:

> We know from research that the "empty vessel approach," the "turn on the faucet and fill the heads of students" approach to teaching and learning, shows little evidence of sustained learning. The teacher may feel good that he or she has managed to get through so much stuff in so little time, but how much actually stuck? And for how long? (p. 62)

In light of this reality, we need to structure curriculum narratives to provide an engaging storyline in which students regularly process new knowledge with their past experiences to deepen or challenge their connections and intensify memory building.

Neuro-economist Paul Zak (2015) observes that narratives not only cause us to pay attention as we become emotionally invested but can also move us to action. In "Why Do Our Brains Demand a Narrative?" (Kelly, n.d.), Zak notes that stories physically change the way the brain is working and that when you're in this changed state, it's possible to change your life experiences. In fact, researchers (Martinez-Conde et al., 2019) confirm that "storytelling engages not just people's intellect but also their feelings. . . . Thus, eliciting emotional arousal likely improves the odds that listeners will not only engage with the material, but also act on it as a result" (p. 8286).

Author Jeremy Adam Smith (2016) arrives at a similar conclusion:

> Study after study after study finds that stories are far more persuasive than just stating the facts. For example, one found that a storytelling approach was more effective in convincing African Americans at risk for hypertension to change their behavior and reduce their blood pressure [see *ScienceDaily*, 2011]. A study of low-performing science students found that reading stories of the struggles of famous scientists led to better grades [see Newman, 2016]. A paper published last year found that witnessing acts of altruism and heroism in films led to more giving in real life [see Suttie, 2015]. (para. 35)

If the narrative has a driving point, a predictable storytelling structure, a relatable character pursuing a goal, and difficult obstacles to surmount that can transform that character, students are more likely to remember what happened because of their active role as listeners. A good story reels us in and stays with us. Listeners make assumptions, seek to confirm predictions, and become invested in the perspective of another, which can influence their own behavior and actions. Not only does this connection make learning "sticky" (more likely to become durable memory), but it can also lead to deeper and more memorable learning as evidenced in authentic assessments. In Episode 7, we will delve deeper into such assessments and demonstrations of learning.

EXAMINE

When learners are connected to the narrative, when they have a reason to care about what happens, information can flow in more readily and students become active sense makers with us as the storyline progresses.

But how exactly do the connections we develop through narrative prompt learner engagement? As creative writers of curriculum, we can visually show the storyline of a course, with the clear goal of inviting our students to *see* and *interpret* the narrative in their own words. We're asking students for evidence that they not only follow the plot, turning points, key individuals, events, concepts, and their connection to one another over time, but also form their own interpretations. We're inviting students to care.

A Preview of the Storyboarding Process

Storyboarding is a clear and accessible strategy to clarify narrative throughlines. A straightforward definition is helpful here. A *storyboard* is a graphic portrayal of a narrative, concept, or script divided into sequential scenes or panels (Sapega, 2021). Students may be aware that storyboards are used in a wide range of fields—in business, publishing, the arts, and media making—to plot out steps and sequence. For example, filmmakers use a storyboard to block out and connect the scenes and narrative; it's a graphic representation of how a video will unfold, shot by shot. The term *storyboard* was developed at the Walt Disney Studio during the 1930s by the animator Webb Smith. Walt Disney believed it was essential for his studio to maintain a careful layout of the stories to ensure the storyline gave readers a reason to care about the characters (Finch, 1995).

To be clear, there's a difference between creating a storyboard for a film and creating one for a curriculum. The filmmaker doesn't know who will see their film; courageously, they create it and cast it out into the world. The impact it will have is never certain. On the other hand, the curriculum narrative is designed for specific students in specific settings with the aim of developing them into capable human beings fulfilling purposeful roles. As a teacher, you will continue to revise your curriculum storyboard on the basis of the students in front of you, their questions and responses, contemporary issues that arise, new resources that become available, and other considerations.

We define *curriculum storyboarding* as using both graphic elements and student-facing language to present an overview of a unit or other course of study that clarifies the connections between unit's components and tells an engaging story of the learning ahead.

Our curriculum work is comparable to a professional animation or film storyboard; we consider the story arc of a course, understanding that the learner needs to care about the journey. To that end, we developed a streamlined storyboard template grounded in our decades-long focus on curriculum mapping, on storytelling as a brain-friendly construct, on personalized learning, and on cultivating dispositions where students see themselves in the story.

As you survey the two storyboard examples that follow, reflect on these questions:

- What do you notice about how the story is being told? How do tone, language, and images clarify the content?
- What do you imagine a student might feel or think after previewing the story at the start of the school year?
- As you consider the students you know, what questions do you hope they might ask?
- How might you use the threads of the curriculum narrative as you move from one unit to the next?
- How might your students interact with the story and be inspired to raise questions or areas of wonder to pursue later on?

Our first example is presented in Figure 4.1—a 5th grade science curriculum laid out as a storyboard. The *unit titles* listed—such as "Force, Motion, Energy: Whee! Energy Causes Motion"—correspond to specific timeframes for implementation. The *image cue* captures the student's attention and visually connects to a concept in the unit. The image cue could be a photo, a painting, a chart, or an icon. The *focus of the story* for each unit is written in one or two sentences. Noteworthy is the way each unit connects to the previous one. Creating throughlines across the storyboard is at the heart of constructing a meaningful narrative that will have staying power for the learner. The storyboard provides a thumbnail that gets at the essence of what the learner will encounter on this stop along the curriculum journey, and it's written in language that's accessible and engaging for learners and their families.

Storyboard Narrative Versus Course Coverage

A narrative approach to curriculum places an active learner at the center. In contrast, the coverage model, often referred to as *drive-by instruction,* tends to promote passivity and compliance. Randy Olson (2015), a science professor turned Hollywood film writer and director turned science communication guru, would likely identify that drive-by coverage of topics follow the AAA structure (i.e., *and . . . and . . . and . . .*) rather than the timeless narrative structure of ABT (i.e., *and . . . but . . . therefore . . .*). Drive-by instruction has the teacher barreling down the road, covering a lot of territory quickly. The student is in the backseat of the car, looking out the window. Although the teacher hopes the student will see key landmarks along the way, it's more likely the student, preoccupied with other matters, will only be looking up

FIGURE 4.1

Curriculum Storyboards: Science

Grade 5 Science

Essential Question(s) How can energy be transformed? How can energy cause matter to transform?

QUARTER 1

Force, Motion, Energy: Whee! Energy causes motion.

THE FOCUS OF THE STORY

Roller coasters and F-18s move fast, but how? We will explore how forces transfer energy, and what happens to an object's motion when multiple forces act upon it. We will ask questions, investigate, and analyze data to make sense of motion.

LEARNING TARGETS

I can ask questions about how energy works through forces to move objects.

I can plan and conduct an experiment to determine the effects of the net force acting on an object.

I can collect and interpret data related to force and the motion of objects.

QUARTER 2

Matter: Whoa! Energy causes matter to change!

THE FOCUS OF THE STORY

What exactly is matter, and what happens to it when it's combined or heated? We will investigate this question and then use what we learn to solve real-world problems.

LEARNING TARGETS

I can construct a simple model to show that matter is composed of atoms.

I can solve a problem by designing a process to separate two or more types of matter within a mixture.

I can use data to show what happens when energy causes a phase change.

QUARTER 2

Electricity: Wait! Energy is useful, but limited.

THE FOCUS OF THE STORY

We know what energy is, but how can it be transformed into electricity so that we can use it? We will explore relationships between electricity and energy, and then consider how to use our data to find creative solutions to problems.

LEARNING TARGETS

I can explain the relationship between energy, electricity, and magnetism.

I can design a solution to a problem using what I know about electricity and electromagnets.

I can use data to determine solutions for conserving energy.

QUARTER 3

Sound and Light: Wow! Energy exists in many forms.

THE FOCUS OF THE STORY

Sound and light seem so very different, but are they? We will ask questions and investigate the ways sound and light travel. Then, we will use what we know to determine how sound and light can help us do work and solve problems.

LEARNING TARGETS

I can identify ways that sound and light are similar and different.

I can use a design process to solve a problem using what I know about sound and light.

I can use observations and data to support conclusions about how sound and light travel.

QUARTER 4

Earth's Structures: What? Energy causes matter to transform.

THE FOCUS OF THE STORY

Is Earth's energy really causing the ground we stand on every day to change? We will study Earth's internal energy and explore how it impacts Earth's structures. We will then consider how to mitigate those changes to reduce the impacts.

LEARNING TARGETS

I can use models to show the structure of Earth and how Earth's crust moves and changes.

I can classify rocks based on how they were formed.

I can describe the relationship between Earth's energy and the forces which cause change on Earth's surfaces.

Source: Virginia Beach City Public Schools, Virginia Beach, Virginia. Used with permission.

and taking note on occasion. In his book, *Houston, We Have a Narrative: Why Science Needs Story* (2015), Olson shares why the ABT structure trumps the AAA structure:

> How important is it for you not just to be understood with a simple AAA presentation but to actually engross, entertain, provoke, and engage an audience from start to finish with the power of narrative using the ABT structure? It's a serious question, and in the past the answer unfortunately has been, "We don't care enough to feel it's worth the time and the energy." But increasingly the answer these days is indeed, "Yes, let's do it," as scientists discover the power and importance of narrative. You just have to know it doesn't come quickly and easily. You get what you pay for. (p. 156)

In a learning narrative, although the teacher is still driving, the student is right there in the front seat, playing an active role in navigation. The pathway laid out is of genuine interest and keeps the student focused. A story emerges from the journey as the student notes the experiences and markers along the way in the storyboard. Surprises will occur as the student *discovers* (as opposed to *covers*) new routes and stops.

Leslie Dietiker (2013), an associate professor of mathematics, examines how mathematics would benefit if teachers would lay it out as a narrative with a story arc that shows how events affect one another through "a chronological experiential layer similar to that of a literary story" (p. 15). She elaborates,

> Distinguishing points along the sequence are changes and transitions of the mathematical states of these ideas. Since literary events are changes through a story, likewise a mathematical event can be conceptualized as a transition of one mathematical event to another. (p. 15)

The key here is that a mathematical story arc should accentuate the connections—not coverage. Let's look at an Algebra I example developed in Little Elm ISD (see Figure 4.2). When Allison worked with this curriculum designer, she first laid out the unit topics over the course of each semester. Second, she identified the primary standards (TEKS). We then engaged in a conversation about how she would clarify with students the significance of each topic—looking for a metaphor, illustration, or application that could drive selection of the playful images, compelling questions, and accessible language.

FIGURE 4.2

Curriculum Storyboards: Algebra 1

Algebra 1

Essential Question(s)
How can we represent real-life situations using a mathematical model?
How can we use these models to make predictions about our future?

3 WEEKS | QUARTER 1

Equations & Inequalities: A Deliberate Balancing Act

THE FOCUS OF THE STORY

Solving for an unknown value is the most fundamental purpose of mathematics. In this unit, students will become adept at manipulating equations and inequalities in order to isolate a variable and gain the ability to solve the mysteries of the unknown.

TEKS

A.5A, A.5B, A.12E

3 WEEKS | QUARTER 1

Functions & Relations: The Power of Predictable Change

THE FOCUS OF THE STORY

How can you gain control over the relationship between independence and dependence? From calculating the cost of an Uber to programming the orbit of the satellites our cell phones depend on, functions provide systematic order in a world that otherwise would be ruled by chaos.

TEKS

A.2A, A.12A, A.12B

3 WEEKS | QUARTER 2

Linear Equations: Predictable Outcomes to Earning Money

THE FOCUS OF THE STORY

In this unit, we apply what we learned in the first quarter to investigate real-world situations that can be represented by predictable patterns. At the conclusion of this unit, you will confidently be able to make predictions that will have a significant effect on your future earnings and protect your financial ventures.

TEKS

A.2B, A.2C, A.2H, A.3A, A.3B, A.3C, A.3D

3 WEEKS | QUARTER 2

Applying Linear Relationships: The Potential to Model Real-World Relations

THE FOCUS OF THE STORY

Can you control time by altering your speed? In this unit, we will explore the effects that one component of a relationship has on another. You will have the opportunity to experience how you can gain control over specific situations that contain two elements with a linear relationship.

TEKS

A.2D, A.2E, A.2F, A.2G, A.3E, A.4A, A.4B, A.4C

3 WEEKS | QUARTER 2

Systems of Linear Equations & Inequalities: Being a Savvy Consumer

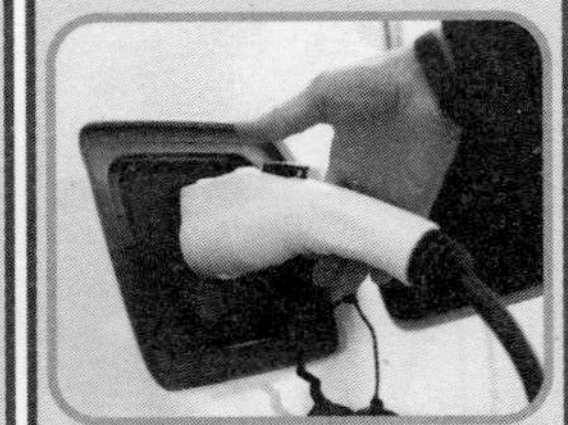

THE FOCUS OF THE STORY

Prepare to level up! In the previous unit, we were able to explore linear relationships and see the effect that one variable can have on another. Now, we expand the situation to include even more unknowns and find the answers to such questions as: Is an EV the best option for our environment? Is it the best option for your wallet?

TEKS

A.2I, A.3F, A.3G A.3H, A.5C

Source: Little Elm Independent School District, Little Elm, Texas. Used with permission.

The use of a narrative structure is relevant regardless of discipline. If the goal is for learners to think, argue, reason, and remember, facts alone (that "and . . . and . . . and" structure again) are not enough. As rhetoricians have noted, "Truths cannot walk on their own legs. They must be carried by people to other people. They must be explained, defended, and spread through language, argument, and appeal" (Campbell et al., 2015, p. 2).

ACT

The curriculum writer can take purposeful actions when crafting a curriculum narrative. Analogous to a creative writer making choices in order to communicate specific messages to readers, a teacher can deliberately craft learning narratives to resonate with students and the lives they lead. Lisa Cron (2013) reminds us to identify the story's point and then use it to guide the narrative's development:

> As the inspiring teacher I've been working with recently asked of a group of rapt 1st graders, "When your mom tells you you're going on vacation, what's the first question you ask?" They all grinned; this was an easy question. "Where are we going!" they chimed.
>
> "Yeah," one earnest little boy said, "Otherwise, how will you know what to pack?"
>
> Indeed.
>
> Same with a story. "What's the point?" equals "Where are we going?" If you don't know it from the beginning, how can you craft a story that will take you there? And, even more important, encourage your reader to come along for the ride?
>
> Just think of your readers as that class of eager six-year-olds. Their first question (read: *your* first question, before you begin to write) will always be: *And so? Where are we going?* (paras. 20–26)

Playing with Design

If you're already intrigued with the concept, it's time to take a risk—to be playful, to think flexibly. Shut down the editorial part of your brain for a moment, and just play with the ideas and possibilities that follow.

Use a story spine.

A *story spine* is a structure that helps you organize and tell a story. Try some first-draft thinking by identifying the following:

- *The beginning:* What frames the problem, issue, or obstacle.
- *The middle:* What engages the learner in the pursuit of a solution or creation.
- *The end:* How a solution or creation affects others and the learner.

Or, for a more playful tone, use Pixar Animation's story spine (see Peters, 2018) to generate and refine your storylines:

- *Once upon a time...*
- *And then one day...* (repeat as necessary)
- *Because of that...* (repeat as necessary)
- *Until finally...*
- *And ever since then...*

One more option is the ABT sentence template offered by scientist/Hollywood writer/director Randy Olson (2015):

> And ____________________, but ______________. Therefore, ________________.
> Another way to describe the narrative arc: Situation (we have this AND this AND this . . .), complication (BUT a problem has arisen with this), resolution (THEREFORE we solved it by doing this). (p. 101)

Olson notes that this template reflects how virtually every science paper is written: "Introduction (And), Method and Results (But), and a Discussion (Therefore)" (p. 6).

Craft the story arc.

Think of a story arc as that which resonates. We're drawn into the plot, and we interact with the characters; the arc drives our motivation as the action builds up to a turning point in the story. That instills remembrance. Similarly, if the student is "following" the plot of a course you've laid out, then you've drawn them into the narrative. Here are some examples:

- In a 3rd grade examination of how the layers of the Earth reveal our planet's history, the students become geologists who are learning about the Earth's crust, mantle, inner core, and outer core and gathering evidence to support their views.

- Middle school science students engaged in a year-long biology course are noting all the conceptual milestones along the way. They can tell the story of how cell structure and organelles connect to mitosis and genetics.
- When a group of high school juniors can articulate the influence of the ancient Greeks on our lives today, they're building a plot line based on their ability to find the throughline from the past to the present.

Ultimately, the essence of learning is the ability of learners to create meaning by making connections among the various experiences they've encountered and retell the story. Plotting the arc of the curriculum narrative is the heart of the story.

Determine the point of view.

Every story has a point of view, and this perspective conveys a set of values as the story unfolds. In the same way, a curriculum presents a certain viewpoint, regardless of whether it has been written in narrative form or not. That viewpoint reveals itself in the resources selected, the assignments designed, and the questions asked. For example,

- A history curriculum might be written from a chronological or a thematic point of view. Or the pace may vary. For instance, the curriculum may slow down to enable students to investigate a range of voices; by doing so, they learn to regularly investigate *what really happened*. This would necessarily involve a complexity of information that goes beyond what textbooks typically offer.
- A math curriculum narrative could be written through a visual arts lens, where students make sense of how shapes and attributes can serve as the basis of art and architecture. Or it could be written using a social justice lens, where students examine case studies on such topics as incarceration rates, education funding, the wage gap between men and women, and the treatment of migrants.
- In a literature class, an English teacher might choose to focus on the voices of women, with readings filtered through the lens of selected female authors.
- A culinary arts narrative could focus on menu development. For example, limited access to food at home can contribute to eating highly processed,

shelf-stable food, and inexpensive menu items at fast-food restaurants often cater to satisfaction rather than nutrition. A narrative could explore students' eating habits and produce recipes that are both soul-satisfying and nutritious.

Of course, specific units will likely have their own specific perspectives for the course of the year.

Jot down ideas (in phrases or images) that capture, stimulate, and unearth joy, wonder, and fascination.

During our workshops, when we share a preview of completed curriculum storyboards like the ones in Figures 4.1 and 4.2, people are immediately smitten with what they see. This curriculum design work is a balance of play, flexibility, creativity, and challenge. By working to tell the story, you may find new insights, discover what really matters, and have a little fun.

Reserve space for student interaction and discovery.

Remain open to continuous learning by modifying the curriculum story on the basis of student interactions. Provide a reflection place and time for students to share how *what* they're learning is affecting *how* they see themselves in the world and in the world of your classroom. It may be helpful to offer reflective prompts to get them going:

- The patterns or connections I'm starting to see are . . .
- Where I still feel lost is . . .
- I wish we could have spent more time exploring the following issues . . .

This regular space to reflect emphasizes the importance of *students as storytellers* as they continue to articulate how this interactive curriculum storyline has influenced them as they progress in their learning journey. The power of these reflections can personalize the experience. For example, a student who wonders about increased local flooding resulting from increased severe weather might design an independent action research project, network with experts from the community, or bring in more resources to highlight the local impact of climate change. Teachers can develop these areas *with* the students rather than *for* the students.

In Our Next Episode . . .

The first four episodes of this book have focused on shifting to a more fluid and streamlined curricular narrative that enables the learner to interact with a pathway of ideas and concepts. Such a curriculum promotes fluidity, creates more cognitive connections, has elegance, and reaches the audience with staying power. The objective is to focus students' attention so that they *see themselves in the narrative*—as curators and creators, as problem solvers and change agents. We're about to take a deeper dive into the creative design choices a curriculum writer makes as the composer of the narrative for particular courses, units, and learning experiences.

Episode 5

Using the Setting to Streamline the Narrative

Learning Target	Engage	Examine	Act
We can select the setting to frame the curriculum narrative.	Explore framing the setting using a disciplinary, an interdisciplinary, and a phenomena-based curricular approach.	Analyze and reflect on how varied curricular settings can open up fresh possibilities.	Identify opportunities to reframe the storyline using a blend of disciplinary, interdisciplinary, and phenomena-based settings.

ENGAGE

A central tenet of writing is revision, which comes from the Latin *revisere*—to see again. Writers know that a draft is where the shaping and reshaping occur. Likewise, given that knowledge never stops growing, curriculum on any subject will never be "finished." Perhaps we might think of curriculum as *perpetual drafts* that we're always revisiting and improving.

For curriculum writers, setting, genre, authentic assessment, and composition are powerful and often unexamined design choices that have a significant effect on learner engagement. This episode focuses on the first of these design choices—namely, *setting*, which we can approach from three narrative perspectives:

- *Disciplinary:* Organized by subject area or field of study
- *Interdisciplinary:* Organized by a common area of focus, such as a theme or an issue
- *Phenomena based:* Organized by an emergent issue or experience

For example, a 2nd grade teacher might begin by focusing on a *disciplinary* approach to a math unit on measurement, engaging students with the terms, tools, and types of measurement dealing with length, weight, and distance. The teacher might then move on to an *interdisciplinary* unit, "On-the-Job Measurement in Our Town." In it, students will apply their newly honed measurement skills and interview different members of the community to see how they use measurement in an array of settings, from the library to the local café to the grocery store. As the end of the school year approaches, the class learns about some upcoming changes in their local train station's schedule and fares, and they elect to investigate how these changes will affect commuters. The teacher launches a *phenomena-based* exploration, "Miles and Miles of Measurement at Our Station."

If teachers select the apt setting to propel a course or unit of study, a streamlined and coherent curriculum naturally unfolds. If, on the other hand, they give minimal attention to the setting and just fall back on *this is the way we've always taught it,* they're more likely to end up with a cumbersome, routinized curriculum.

As a curriculum writer, when you select the setting, you launch the learning narrative. The setting puts the story in motion, streamlines the action, and sets the stage for the action of the learners. However, this has real implications for schools and how they might plan their programs to accommodate disciplinary, interdisciplinary, and phenomena-based approaches. As we look at each of those setting choices, we'll lay out some implications in terms of four programmatic structures in schools: schedules, learning spaces, student grouping patterns, and the corresponding grouping of personnel. The goal is to open up dialogues among siloed departments and school institutional groups (such as human resources, information technology, and family outreach) in service to modern learner goals and pedagogy.

Discipline-Based Curriculum Settings

For better or worse, a classical disciplinary approach—built on language arts, mathematics, social studies, science, world language, performing arts, visual arts, career and technical education, and physical education—is entrenched in our schooling system. These disciplines affect institutions in terms of teacher credentialing and certification, and they're embedded in school life and structures in the sense that schools allot specific times in their schedule to focus on the perspectives, knowledge, and problem-solving approaches in each specific subject area. For example, a middle school science teacher might implement a three-week unit on human systems to address a biological inquiry from the Next Generation Science Standards: *Students will investigate organisms as biologists using the skills, the tools, and the models of science.*

There is great value in a classical learning setting built on an immersion in the discipline of science. However, discipline-based curricular settings do present several key challenges:

- **The automaticity implicit in a system of organizing learning, developing texts, and cultivating routines can stymie creativity.** It's easy to slip into "coverage" of curriculum with this model.
- **It can be difficult to stay fresh and commit to being current.** New knowledge is growing exponentially, and old curricula may have no room to include this information. This means teachers are continually determining what *not* to study in a subject.
- **Program structures are frequently designed to perpetuate the classical subject areas as rigid silos.** For example, most high school teachers are certified in a subject area, meet in their department with other

specialists in their subject area, teach students who are grouped together for that subject area, and move those students from course to course adhering to a highly regulated and rigid time frame. It's the exposure model. Although the dominance of rigid schedules permeates our schools, offering new possibilities for better uses of time with the disciplinary approach will better serve learners.

Interdisciplinary Curriculum Settings

When teachers bring two or more disciplines together to examine a common focus area, it's interdisciplinary. For example, a 4th grade class is studying flight from scientific, literary, artistic, and historical perspectives in addressing the following questions: *What flies? Have human beings always wanted to fly? Why do we fly? How does flight affect our lives?* A well-designed interdisciplinary unit reveals that all applications of knowledge and skills are inherently interdisciplinary.

There are two primary challenges to interdisciplinary design:

- **Not everything we study has natural interdisciplinary connections.** Forcing a fit for the sake of an interdisciplinary approach often results in one subject assuming the leading role, or it becomes a shallow exploration where students struggle to see the benefits of looking for those connections.
- **Schools that run on a traditional curriculum pacing calendar may perceive that an interdisciplinary approach will take students "off course."** This fear is exaggerated. For example, elementary teachers generally have a great deal of control over how to create links among subjects because they often teach almost all of them. High schools and middle schools that share the same learner groupings and have concurrent time frames will find it much easier to formulate these units, which is why "houses" and grade-level teams tend to flourish with interdisciplinary design.

Phenomena-Based Curriculum Settings

These involve learner-generated inquiries into specific phenomena. External phenomena could be an event, an issue, a setting, a situation, or a discovery that is current and relevant to the learner. Internal phenomena are generated by a learner's inner life—and can also be an event, an issue, a situation, a discovery, or a feeling that is relevant and timely for the learner. Unlike predetermined curriculum experiences, a phenomena-based topic is not preplanned; experiences emerge naturally and reveal the notion of immediacy. For example, when brushfires sweep through an area in Southern California, a group of local high school students might want to investigate why. They might decide to globalize the investigation and examine the approaches taken in other communities that have similar concerns about wildfires, such as Melbourne, Australia. Or take the case of a 10-year-old who has moved to a new school and is filled with a wide range of emotions as she makes the transition. She may wish to communicate her experience to her new classmates. What strikes us as important here is that students are well-versed in how to initiate a quest to explore—and that they can do so with the support of their teachers.

Three challenges with a phenomena-based setting may immediately come to mind:

- **The grip of a discipline-based curriculum model conflicts with emergent interests and "in the moment" learning opportunities.** What gets measured often matters most. If your school's achievement metrics are discipline-specific with limited real-world applications, there will likely be significant resistance to use of phenomena-based settings.
- **Relegating phenomena-based curricular topics as an "extra" exacerbates unequal access to learning opportunities.** Only some students may be able to take advantage of these co-curricular experiences or individual quests; a substantial number will likely miss out on opportunities to engage with complex, ambiguous issues. Key in most school settings will be transitioning to making these experiences more routine.
- **Some students will struggle with learner-generated inquiries.** Students will have more quality experiences in this type of learning if the teacher explores beforehand with students how and when to initiate an experience.
- **Schedules for both students and teachers will need to be flexible to support the planning for and execution of learner-generated inquiries**. Learning spaces for independent work, small-group sharing, possibly off-campus visits, and virtual interactions are optimal. Teachers

might serve as sponsors to groups or individuals in quests when their subject-matter expertise is of most assistance. Teachers might group students with others who have like-minded interests within or between grade levels. The approach has power because learners can actually apply their learning. It's not just preparation for life beyond school; rather, students are engaging in life experiences *of their choosing*. Confidence and curiosity are potential outcomes for the learner.

EXAMINE

Illustrating the three curricular approaches as *settings* begins to frame how to integrate learning experiences to grow independent learners who are curious about the world, who investigate challenges, who develop ideas, and who share those ideas with others. Figure 5.1 lists topics in science (animal habitats), mathematics (measurement), and history (the American Revolution). We see how the topics broaden as they move into an interdisciplinary or a phenomena-based setting.

There are several crucial factors in the design of the curriculum narrative: the driving purpose, standards and goals, the basis for the storyline, teacher roles, and student roles. Figure 5.2 defines each of these factors in terms of the three curricular settings. As you review this figure, reflect on your curriculum and on how you might refine current approaches and expand possibilities.

FIGURE 5.1

Topical Examples in Three Curricular Settings

Discipline Based	Interdisciplinary	Phenomena Based
Animal Habitats	Adaptation	How can we support the animals in our schoolyard habitat?
Measurement	Measurement on the Job and in the World	Predicting the impact of the next hurricane and how we can respond
The American Revolution	Upheavals: Revolutions in Every Field	Personal revolutions: The experiences that have changed my perspective

FIGURE 5.2

Design Criteria in Three Curricular Settings

Criteria	Discipline Based	Interdisciplinary	Phenomena/Learner Generated
Driving Purpose	Focuses on what it means to be learned, literate, and skillful in the subject. Students learn to become active representatives of a field. They take on such roles as historian, artist, and mathematician.	Focuses on expanding multiple perspectives in the examination of themes, issues, and problems to deepen learning.	Focuses on a thoughtful exploration of emergent phenomena in the student's world. Students learn how to initiate a quest to explore a current idea or problem, whether it's personal, local, or global.
Standards and Goals	The teacher sorts subject-area expectations to prioritize what is most essential.	The teacher includes essential subject-area expectations in related subjects and cross-disciplinary practices.	The teacher identifies long-term goals and subject-area expectations, as well as the authentic assessments that emerge.
Basis for Storyline	The storyline is generated to include the requisite layouts of the discipline, combined with inquiry opportunities.	The storyline is generated to weave together perspectives from the various disciplines, combined with inquiry opportunities.	The storyline evolves based on the topic or nature of the exploration. The storyline cannot be drafted ahead of time and requires a "right now" designer.
Teacher Roles	• The *teacher as designer* makes daily choices about what to cover and uncover. • The *teacher as tour guide* leads in introducing and exploring key topics. • The *teacher as mentor* facilitates exploration, investigation, and analysis so students can see varied approaches and perspectives. • The *teacher as coach* promotes independent work on assignments. The teacher observes, redirects, gives feedback, and encourages students to pause for reflection and analysis. • The *teacher as partner* demonstrates ongoing commitment to each student's success.	• The *teacher as designer* makes purposeful linkages to illustrate the interconnections among themes, problems, issues, or topics. • The *teacher as instructor* searches for connections and leads in introducing and exploring key topics. • The *teacher as mentor* facilitates student exploration, investigation, and analysis so students can see varied approaches, perspectives, and ways of thinking. • The *teacher as coach* promotes independent work on assignments. The teacher observes, redirects, gives feedback, and encourages students to pause for reflection and analysis.	• The *teacher as networker* seeks out expertise to inform and interact with students and seeks out opportunities for students to share their learning. • The *teacher as coach* promotes independent work on assignments. The teacher observes, probes thinking, gives feedback, and encourages students to pause for reflection and analysis.
Student Roles	Student as knowledge constructor and creator	Student as knowledge constructor and creator	Student as inquirer, self-navigator, knowledge constructor, creator, and change agent

What does this look like in practice? Are these changes viable? For insight, we reached out to Eric Chagala, principal of the internationally recognized Vista Innovation & Design Academy (VIDA) in Vista Unified Schools, California. VIDA is a public middle school that transformed itself by using the Stanford d. School's design thinking process and emphasizing deep empathy work. Here's what Eric shared about VIDA's approach:

> Our founding faculty used interviews with students, alumni, parents, and one another to establish what we would do. When we coded the qualitative information, it spoke to students' struggle to see themselves in the school and in the learning environment. In response, we revised our approach to how we set up and offered classes. Along with a brand-new pedagogy using problem-based learning as a framework for integrating design thinking into all classes, our North Star became using engagement as the first intervention for all students.
>
> But school transformation does not solely pivot on what is offered for students. We took a bigger and broader swing—aiming to engage the hearts and minds of both students *and* faculty. We set out to honor our staff's humanity, and one of the leading mantras for that effort was this question: *What have you always wanted to do with students that you have never been able to do?*
>
> School leadership worked to turn those lost "wants" into brand-new, specialized elective classes and other on-campus opportunities to connect with the strengths, interests, and values of teachers as well as students. The only constraints we placed on these classes were that they needed to intentionally foster the creativity of students, provide a technical skill students could leverage for innovation, or go deeper into our design thinking process. The way these classes, which we call "Design Labs," work is that students are offered a list of choices by grade level, and they are almost guaranteed to be given one of their top three interests each semester. Teachers have a chance to work alongside students, in ways and with content that feeds their soul. Student sign-ups help drive what we actually offer, and because of this, new classes rotate in and out of our line-up every year.
>
> What may be even more important about these classes is the intentional way we've incorporated them into the school schedule. Students attend core classes plus PE on a rotating A/B block schedule, meeting three times a week. But because the Design Lab classes are at the heart of our school, we have divided one 90-minute block period so that students spend 40 minutes at lunch and 50 minutes in Design Lab every single day [see Figure 5.3]. Attaching these classes to the

FIGURE 5.3

Design Labs Offered at Vista Innovation Design School

Design Labs:		
Foster Creativity, Build Skill & Design Thinking		
3-D Sculpture	Comedy Sketch Design	Psychology
Animatronics	Robotics (VEX)	NASA & Space Exploration
Collage Creations	SeaPerch (Underwater Robotics)	Medical Detectives (Project Lead the Way)
Cryptozoology	Curiosity Hacked (Art & Coding)	CSI (Project Lead the Way)
Music Composition	Engineering 101	Grain Creations
Game Design	Flight, RC Car & Rocketry	Toy Story Animations
Pinterest Designs	Architecture Design (Project Lead the Way)	Let's Get Cooking
Jewelry Design	Digital Fabrication	Wildlife Versus Extinction
Screen Writing	Fabric Design	Interior Design
eSports (Data Science)	Critical Hits (Video Game Music)	Survivor

Source: Vista Innovation and Design Academy, Vista, California. Used with permission.

lunch period ensures that every single student, regardless of any complicating factors, gets these engaging, spirit-filling experiences on a daily basis. No one can ever take it away from them.

Every three years, we reach out to students for direct input into topics that interest and excite them. It feeds administrator and faculty creativity, challenging us to match teacher interest and expertise to student-generated content we never would have come up with on our own. (Personal communication February 2, 2023)

ACT

Selecting a setting that best supports the narrative is an essential element of streamlining because it promotes coherence and clarity. For example, a 1st grade class might read Theo Guidone's *Drum City,* where one boy's drumming on a kettle initiates a community response. The teacher could choose an interdisciplinary experience that encompasses music, English language arts, and science and begin with a question like *What everyday items did people in the book use as an instrument?* Students would learn about the parts of musical instruments and use their drawing skills to design a musical instrument of their choice. A phenomena-based learning experience might focus on how to produce and play musical instruments from standard junkyard or recycled materials. Just consider the possibilities. No one setting is better than the others, but having students consistently engage in all three is better aligned with modern learner goals and pedagogy.

To take action in setting selection, we suggest the following steps.

Step 1: Review the setting options.

Begin by reviewing the characteristics of disciplinary, interdisciplinary, and phenomena-based settings to see how they will affect the narrative flow and storyboard. If possible, encourage a discussion with colleagues to ensure clarity about each setting:

- **A disciplinary setting.** Generate the storyline on the basis of the requirements of the discipline, combined with inquiry opportunities. Make thoughtful and deliberate connections among the units across the year to avoid isolated "stops" along the journey. By emphasizing the connections, learners are more likely to find them and be able to "tell the story." For example, a 5th grader midway through the school year might tell the story of how, in math class, he started by understanding the place value system and then moved to grasping the concepts of number lines, then decimal points, and then negative numbers to the hundredths place.
- **An interdisciplinary setting.** Generate the storyline for a project, unit, or year by weaving together perspectives from disciplines, combined with inquiry opportunities. This narrative best follows an inquiry sequence rooted in essential questions, such as *How does what I put into my body affect the way it works?*
- **A phenomena-based setting.** Here, a curriculum storyline evolves on the basis of the topic of exploration. It cannot be drafted ahead of time; learners are the storytellers here, and the storyline follows their journey. For example, students might ask questions like *Is there life on other planets? How do I make a better lunch box to keep things cold? How long does it take to get an ambulance in my neighborhood, and how does that compare to surrounding neighborhoods?*

Questions to reflect on: What is the effect of each storyline on our course? How do they differ from one another? What is the value of each?

Step 2: Choose the setting that best serves the narrative.

Review your existing course and determine which setting is the best match for your identified narrative. Step back and reflect on whether another setting might improve the impact of the course or unit. For example, a high school World History teacher might consider whether it is better to concentrate on the historical facts of the French Revolution and keep the unit within the discipline's existing setting or pursue a deeper understanding of the period's events within an interdisciplinary setting by collaborating with an English teacher on a concurrent reading of *A Tale of Two Cities.*
Questions to reflect on: What is the existing setting? Have you taught this course or unit using a setting you selected on the basis of habit? Does it engage students? What might happen if you switched from the existing setting to a different one?

Step 3: Find opportunities to employ the *other* settings.

Search for spots in the curriculum where you might create space in the curriculum for settings you *didn't* choose. For example, if high school history and English teachers decide to forgo a whole-class reading of *A Tale of Two Cities,* they might still offer a range of extension options for the unit—one of which might be reading an array of literary works (including Dickens) that shed light on the realities of the French Revolution.
Question to reflect on: How might we generate and test out new storylines that align with modern learner goals and pedagogy?

In Our Next Episode . . .

This episode focused on identifying your current curriculum setting. Perhaps you mostly rely on a disciplinary approach. Here, we make a case for meaningful learning experiences that integrate interdisciplinary and phenomena-based settings. The goal is to imagine fresh possibilities. Next, we turn to the choice of genre—how you can recast an ordinary topic as a theme, an issue, a problem, or a case study.

Episode 6

Genre Selection: Sketching a Course and Unit Narrative

Learning Target	Engage	Examine	Act
We can generate fresh curriculum possibilities through genre selection in course and unit design.	Look at the effect on curriculum of various genre choices: topics, themes, problems, issues, and case studies.	Analyze genre selections and their effect on content in disciplinary, interdisciplinary, and phenomena-based settings.	Develop fresh possibilities through genre selection and streamline the curriculum content.

ENGAGE

Just as creative writers can choose to give their readers different experiences by presenting work as fiction or nonfiction, poetry, drama, or prose, curriculum writers have genre options too. Framing the genre for a unit of study or for an entire course is a golden opportunity to engage students. The genre serves as a lens through which students will view the inquiry.

Designers can choose among five types of curriculum genre (see Jacobs, 2002; Jacobs & Alcock, 2017):

- **Topic-based units.** Here, the focus is on subjects to explore. Students will seek foundational information. Topics can be people, places, or things, such as snow, insects, San Francisco, Marie Curie, or the periodic table of elements.
- **Theme-based units.** Thematic units are designed around a broad-based concept that promotes insight and connections. They connote ideas, characteristics, and qualities and lean toward more abstract concepts. Examples include patterns, rites of passage, innovation, and favorite places.
- **Problem-based units.** Problem-based units identify a specific problem in a context and develop a solution. Examples include how to start a new business in our community, how to build a footbridge over a stream behind our middle school, and how to create a weather station in our elementary school.
- **Issue-based units.** Inquiries focused on issues are compelling because they examine a controversy that's meant to be explored rather than resolved. The purpose of this kind of unit is to expand viewpoints and find out why people embrace a particular stance. Examples include the voting age, censorship, the death penalty, and dress codes.
- **Case study–based units.** Specific instances, situations, and works are at the heart of case study examinations. The student investigates a specific application to probe deeply, perhaps arriving at broader implications. A case study approach can apply to the study of literature, places, scientific studies, or communities. Examples include Hurricane Ida, the pyramids of Giza, the poem "A Dream Deferred" by Langston Hughes, and the workings of a local fire station.

Why consider genre selection? Because the genre selected has a powerful effect on the types of learning experiences that follow. For example, if a middle school class studies genetic engineering as an *issue-based unit,* resources and activities might focus on the ethics of parents making choices to determine characteristics of their babies. If it's a *topic-based unit,* resources and activities would focus on engaging with and retaining information about, say, the nature of genetics and the development of animal genetic engineering from the 1970s to today. Just to clarify, topic-based units certainly have value when the learning experience is intended to provide background and a foundation, but if we're seeking different types of learning, then we must move to a different genre.

Genre—And the Compelling Narrative

In our curriculum development workshops, we ask teachers to revise an existing course title in view of arriving at a fresher take on the material that's more likely to engage their students. This doesn't mean just renaming the unit; a shift in genre is a shift in form. For example, we might take a middle school science course titled "Solar Energy" and change it to "How to Use Solar Energy to Run Our School." All choices in the unit follow suit; instead of simply collecting topical information on solar energy, students are now collecting information, ideas, and data about the school as well as considering possible solar energy setups, timeframes, budgets, and installation issues and the effect of those choices on the school, community, and environment. It becomes a new unit.

Let's look at how we might reconceive that unit on solar energy, with the five genres in mind:

- Topic-based unit title: "Solar Energy"
- Theme-based unit title: "Sustainability"
- Problem-based unit title: "How to Use Solar Energy to Run Our School"
- Issue-based unit title: "Conservation and Its Impact on Jobs"
- Case study–based unit title: "Biosphere 2: An Earth System Science Research Facility in Arizona"

The genre selection also points directly to *the type of assessment* that will follow. In a topic-based unit on solar energy, the learner might show the gathering and organizing of factual background information on solar energy as evidence of learning.

However, if the focus is issue based—say, in a unit titled "Conservation and Its Impact on Jobs"—students, to show their learning, would need to analyze the range of viewpoints regarding the effect of foresting in a given region, such as in the rainforest near Juneau, Alaska. When students are engaged in the exploration of a theme, such as sustainability, the forms of evidence will look at the effects of sustainability on the environment and on the community's families, businesses, and governance.

Problem-based units are straightforward; the assessment in a unit titled "How to Use Solar Energy to Run Our School" will be a proposed solution to that problem. Thus, students might produce a plan for a solar collector. They might also explore case studies of solar parks, starting with the world's largest—Bhadla Solar Park in India—and continue with a look at local solar energy installations and an evaluation of their effectiveness. We will dive deeper into the design of assessment in the next episode.

EXAMINE

To underscore the effect of genre choice, we'll look at four examples. Two are in disciplinary settings, one is in an interdisciplinary setting, and one is phenomena based. In each instance, teachers have made a genre choice with student engagement in mind.

Genre in a Disciplinary Setting

Figure 6.1 shows a 9th grade English curriculum developed by the Secondary English Team in Texas's Denton Independent School District. Although the curriculum designers were well-versed in backward design, they were intrigued when Allison shared the rationale for (and examples of) the storyboard approach. The English coordinator decided to run with the idea, and within 24 hours a yearlong thematic storyline had taken shape.

As you review the figure, notice how beautifully connected the narrative is from unit to unit: Under Pressure (considering characters in fiction who are under internal and external pressures), Navigating Text Complexities (developing strategies to navigate complex texts), Influence (analyzing the components of effective arguments), Choose Your Adventure (formulating short and extended responses), and Looking Forward (developing a multi-genre project). This 9th grade experience balances

FIGURE 6.1

The Story of English 1

English I

SEMESTER 1 | 9 WEEKS — Under Pressure

THE FOCUS OF THE STORY

Narrative Writing & Literary Analysis in Book Clubs

Freshman year starts with fiction book clubs, providing you with a familiar route into the analysis of literature, specifically by having you analyze the internal and external pressures characters face. Writing several short responses to text, as well as your first narrative or memoir, will give you the opportunity to showcase your writing abilities and participate in rich discussions.

STANDARDS

Related TEKS

SEMESTER 1 | 9 WEEKS — Navigating Text Complexities

THE FOCUS OF THE STORY

Writing in Response to Reading & Literary Analysis of Multigenre Short Texts

Being new to high school, you may not yet be equipped to navigate the kinds of complex literary and nonfiction texts that you will encounter in courses to come. This unit invites you to try out multiple strategies that make navigating complex texts doable. The goal of this unit is to equip you to do the thinking work necessary for understanding, rather than have you abandon difficult texts or rely on teachers for the interpretation.

STANDARDS

Related TEKS

SEMESTER 2 | 6 WEEKS — Influence

THE FOCUS OF THE STORY

Argument Writing & Short Nonfiction Text Analysis

Midyear, you will think about the power of influencers and begin to evaluate the tactics they use in their writing. By questioning intent and breaking down components of effective argument—such as the use of reasoning, facts, and logic—you will see how analyzing authors' techniques will enhance your own ability to argue a point. Using specific texts as models, you will craft multiple arguments in areas you care deeply about.

STANDARDS

Related TEKS

SEMESTER 2 | 6 WEEKS — Choose Your Adventure

THE FOCUS OF THE STORY

Writing in Response to Reading & Literary Analysis of Fiction in Book Clubs

Placed in the third and fourth quarters, this timely unit on the power of response will use dystopian, fantasy, and science fiction novels to revisit fiction. It will have a heavy emphasis on writing short and extended responses. You will engage in book clubs and will also respond to informational texts that cross content areas.

STANDARDS

Related TEKS

SEMESTER 2 | 6 WEEKS — Looking Forward

THE FOCUS OF THE STORY

Informational Writing & Multigenre Research

To close out freshman year, you will look into the future and come up with ideas for a multigenre project. As you research this area, you will tap into your ambitions, goals, or plans and deliver your discoveries in a variety of ways, incorporating four genres in your project. This blend of academic and creative writing will result in personalized projects that showcase your research and writing capabilities. It will be a culmination of the work you have done throughout the year.

STANDARDS

Related TEKS

Source: Denton Independent School District, Denton, Texas. Used with permission.

literacy development, compelling themes, and personalized choices to develop students' skill and agency and promote self-discovery.

The writing style is inviting, designed to hook the learner, and the narrative is anchored in state standards, the Texas Essential Knowledge and Skills (TEKS).

The second storyboard example, shown in Figure 6.2, is from a high school adventure leadership course developed at Colegio Maya de Guatemala. The designer focused on health and well-being as the basis for effective and relational teams.

Genre in an Interdisciplinary Setting

Inspired by the interdisciplinary projects encountered during her work in schools across the United States and overseas, Heidi has composed a set of samples that reflect high-quality, engaging genre titles that inspire students and teachers to work on rigorous and creative projects (see Figure 6.3).

Notice, for example, that grade 6 students explore the role of mosquitoes in spreading disease. They examine a case study on yellow fever, create an informational website about mosquito-borne diseases, study the effect of such diseases in different locations around the world, and investigate the global tire trade as a mechanism for the *worldwide* dispersal of container-breeding mosquitoes. Grade 3 students become soil scientists, examining dirt's composition and its impact on the environment. First graders consider the rainforest both literally and through literature.

Genre in a Phenomena-Based Setting

The power of emergent phenomena-based work is in its immediacy and freshness. Whether the driving interest is personal, local, or global, the connection is right now for the learner. The Organisation for Economic Co-operation and Development (OECD) puts it this way:

> People learn better and become more engaged when the content relates to them, and when they can see the parallels between many global issues and their immediate environment. For example, students can become aware of the risks related to climate change by studying the effects that natural phenomena (e.g., hurricanes, floods) have on their own community. Capitalizing on local expertise and the experience of young people in culturally responsive ways is particularly relevant when teaching less privileged or immigrant youth. (OECD, 2019, p. 172)

FIGURE 6.2

Curriculum Storyboard: Adventure Leadership

Adventure Leadership

Essential Question(s) **How can we become better leaders of ourselves and others?**

3 WEEKS

Creating Community

THE FOCUS OF THE STORY

Our adventure in leadership begins as we come together in the Forming phase of group development as we get to know one another. Each of us has something valuable to contribute to our collective synergy. We create group norms to establish a common expectation for our experiential activities with a hearty dose of play.

7 WEEKS

A High Performing Team

THE FOCUS OF THE STORY

Building upon the Forming, Storming, and Norming phases of the group development process, we move to the High Performance Model. By internally building and reflecting upon individual and group performance, we strive to uplevel as a performing team.

3 WEEKS

Personal Leadership

THE FOCUS OF THE STORY

How do we prefer to lead and be led? Which leadership abilities do each of us target for growth? By examining leadership continuum theory and leadership styles, we experiment and practice leading adventure activities and later recreational activities.

7 WEEKS

Learning to Lead

THE FOCUS OF THE STORY

Transformational leadership from within will support you in spreading your wings to fly in leading. As a blank canvas to experiment and grow leadership practices, our team will first lead cooperative challenge activities within our group. We will progress on to leading activities with other groups within the communities they belong to, whether an athletic team, service project, or church group.

Source: Colegio Maya – American International School of Guatemala, Santa Catarina Pinula, Guatemala. Used with permission.

FIGURE 6.3

Ideas for Interdisciplinary Units in Grades 1, 3, and 6

Grade	Unit Title	Unit Description
Grade 1	*The Great Kapok Tree*	Using research tools and through their observations and investigations, our 1st grade researchers will learn about rainforests across the world. We will focus on four strata: animals, plants, adaptations, and rainforest preservation, which they will consider through the lens of Lynne Cherry's book, *The Great Kapok Tree*. We will create stories about their imagined experience and compile them in a class book called *Our Adventures in the Rainforest!*
Grade 3	Digging up the Dirt on Soil	Our 3rd grade soil scientists will explore the components of soil and the type of soil in different places in the community: at school, in the park, in home gardens, and at a neighboring farm. They will identify and sort different soil types, make observations, and conduct tests to see which soil is best for which plants. We will create a schoolwide compost site to assist with gardening. This will be one aspect of a student-created marketing campaign to reduce trash in the school building.
Grade 6	WANTED: MOSQUITOES! The deadliest animal in the world	Mosquitoes play a significant role in the worldwide spread of diseases. As researchers, we will examine case studies on yellow fever and learn about the scientists who risked their lives fighting this disease. With our developed baseline in infectious diseases, we will create a website that displays basic mosquito-borne disease information, along with brief case studies. Using our apps, we will track global trends and graph the effects of such diseases on human beings in different locations. We will unpack various political and economic perspectives and discuss arguments for and against the global tire trade, which promotes the spread of mosquito-borne diseases.

Take, for example, Egypt's STEM21 schools project (see STEM Egypt, n.d.). Starting in 2012, an international partnership between Egypt's Ministry of Education and USAID designed a school model to develop emerging leaders and innovators who are committed to improving the lives of Egyptian people. Using an engineering design process, Egypt's STEM21 schools are driven by four "grand challenges" the country faces: improving sources of clean water, reducing pollution, improving the use of alternative energies, and reducing population and slums.

During the first two years, coursework focuses on each of the four areas; students learn as they work together to design prototypes and testable simulations. The third year of the program is a capstone year in which students choose which of the four areas they would like to pursue further. High school students from this program have garnered international recognition for their innovations and ideally will fuel scientific invention and generate employment opportunities and economic growth in Egypt. The Egypt STEM21 schools are oriented to the genre of *problem based* to address emerging challenges and provide an opportunity to grow competence and develop actual solutions. Here is a description of these Egyptian STEM schools—and their graduates—from F. Joseph Merlino (2022), president of the 21st Century Partnership for STEM Education:

> The Egyptian integrated curriculum features five semester-long capstone projects involving a design challenge based on one or more grand challenges. The capstones count for 60 percent of a student's course grade. The traditional high-stakes graduation exams have been replaced with a mix of practical assessments, capstones, and tests of conceptual understanding. These Egyptian STEM school students have won many international science and math competitions and gone on to enroll in highly selective U.S., European and Egyptian universities. (p. 2).

As we continue to focus on shifting to a narrative approach to writing curriculum and to humanizing and revitalizing curriculum by capturing emergent learning, consider the following questions:

- How do the genre examples inspire thinking about your curriculum?
- What factors might make it easier for you to apply genre in your curriculum?
- What factors might make it more difficult for you to apply genre in your curriculum?

ACT

How do we create a compelling genre to engage our students? You might be doing this work alone or with a team of teachers. To begin, whether the course at hand is an existing or a new course, it's best to step back, set aside previous approaches, and start with one unit for practice. Use the following steps as a guide:

1. Select a course of study or subject layout.
2. Select *one unit within the course.* It can be disciplinary or interdisciplinary.
3. Determine the unit's current genre. For the record, it's usually topic based.

4. Study the five genres—topics, themes, problems, issues, and case studies—and each genre's accompanying examples.
5. Draft an alternative title for your unit that will better engage students and deepen learning.
6. Share examples with other teachers to inspire creativity and confidence.

Figure 6.4 provides a few before-and-after examples from schools where we have worked. You'll see the original title contrasted with the updated and revised title. For example, the teachers reconceived a 7th grade science unit originally titled "Moon Phases." The revised title and focus? "Howl at the Moon: How Do Moon Phases Influence Animal Behavior?" What student wouldn't be interested in that?

These examples are noteworthy because they encompass all three approaches: disciplinary, interdisciplinary, and phenomena-based explorations. It's liberating when teachers feel they have permission to break out of the shackles of an old-style unit framework and enliven the same content with a fresh take on positioning the content and skills. Genre matters.

In Our Next Episode . . .

With their narrative draft in hand, an author looks it over to see how to improve the storyline to hook the reader's imagination. This episode focused on the second design choice of *genre*. We examined approaches for revising and revitalizing units by shifting the genre format to hook the student's imagination. The next episode will explore not only how to design authentic assessments to evaluate student engagement, but also the overall effect on students of our streamlined curriculum plans.

FIGURE 6.4

Rethinking Genre: Before-and-After Unit Titles

Grade and Course	Original Unit Title	Revised Unit Title
1st Grade	Inferring	Reading Sleuths *Gathering information, making observations, and using schema to make conclusions about what we read*
2nd Grade Math	Personal Financial Literacy	Money Makes the World Go Round
5th Grade English Language Arts	Summarizing Fiction	Why Did This Happen? *Summarizing a text, exploring the events that led to final outcomes, and analyzing where the story could have gone in a different direction*
5th Grade Math and Design	Budgets	Let's Build a House *Discovering our wants and needs when confined to a limit*
5th Grade Math and Science	Volume	Case Study: Amazon, Your Package Has Arrived! *Looking at delivery trucks (how much of a load they can hold in terms of square footage and volume; how items are packed) and at the packaging department (the sizes and shapes of boxes)*
5th Grade Science	Interdependency	Teamwork Makes the Dream Work in the Animal World!
6th Grade English Language Arts	Character Study	What's Their Relationship Status? *How dialogue and actions change character relationships*
7th Grade Science	Moon Phases	Howl at the Moon: How Do Moon Phases Affect Animal Behavior? *Looking at data on campus, such as referrals; at crime data; at historical data; at how other animals respond; and at how other behavioral patterns correspond to moon phase timing. Will examine case studies.*
8th Grade Science	Climatic Interactions	Virtual Field Trip: Exploring How Climate Change Affects Coastlines Using Google Maps
11th Grade U.S. History	The Gilded Age	Corruption, Money, and Scandal: How the Gilded Age Rocked the American Public
11th/12th Grade Family and Consumer Sciences Teacher (FACS)	Social Work and Social Services	It Takes a Village: You Don't Have to Do It on Your Own
High School Biology	Characteristics of Life and Biomolecules	You Are What You Eat: Getting the Most Energy-Efficient Bang for Your Buck
Interventionist: Elementary Science	Plant Life Cycle	Watch Me Grow!

Episode 7

How Authentic Assessments Bolster the Curriculum Narrative

Learning Target	Engage	Examine	Act
We can develop authentic assessments to make a curriculum narrative come alive for learners.	Explore four criteria for authentic assessment.	Examine examples of authentic assessments that enliven the curriculum narrative.	Identify places in the curriculum narrative best suited for authentic assessments and sketch out ideas.

ENGAGE

How do we measure what matters? This episode considers how authentic assessments can measure desired outcomes *and* provide learners with opportunities to engage in complex and interesting challenges that add value to their world.

Tony Wagner and Ted Dintersmith (2015) made a provocative statement that bolstered the case for rethinking assessment in schools: "Our kids spend their formative years preparing for tests, not life. Let's face it: our education system is plagued by inertia—lots of it" (pp. 83–84). More than a quarter-century earlier, Grant Wiggins (1989) also pointed out the need to rethink assessment:

> Students acknowledge this truth with their plaintive query, *Is this going to be on the test?* And their instincts are correct; we should not feel despair about such a view. The test always sets the de facto standards of a school despite whatever else is proclaimed. A school should "teach to the test." The catch is that the test must offer students a genuine intellectual challenge, and teachers must be involved in designing the test if it is to be an effective point of leverage. (p. 704)

The Three Tiers of Assessment

Every field of pursuit has natural pathways to mastery. Inspired by the contributions of Wiggins and McTighe (2005), we reference *three tiers of assessment* (see Figure 7.1).

Predicated on gaining foundational knowledge with the fundamentals, **drill and practice** zooms in on the student's skills. The teacher observes the students on the granular skill level and gives feedback. With teacher guidance, students make adjustments and proceed to independent practice. For example, a budding violinist will receive specific tips from their instructor on fingering, and then they will practice until the next lesson.

With rehearsals or scrimmages, the teacher establishes a simulated situation to pull together various skills for the student to apply in context. Rather than memorizing and then retrieving key facts about historical figures or events as they would in a drill and practice scenario, students would apply what they've learned through analysis of a primary source document or event. The teacher "stops play"

FIGURE 7.1

Three Tiers of Assessment

Drill	Rehearsal or Scrimmage	Authentic Assessment
To assess fundamental skill development or retention of targeted knowledge	To assess students' proficiency drafting or testing out ideas in a simulated context	To assess students' application of learning in a genuine context and place
• Questions that lend themselves to one strategy and one right answer • Selected-response questions • Short-answer questions • Demonstrations of fundamental skills and techniques	• Open-ended problems or prompts that require thinking critically and strategically • Simulated performance or play situation • Draft of justification or explanation, with supporting evidence • Creation of a product with the teacher as primary audience and evaluator • Creation of a performance with the teacher as primary audience and evaluator	• Creation of a product for a target audience, in an authentic context and specific place • Recorded or live performance for a target audience, in an authentic context and specific place • Service delivered to a specific group • Service with an issue-driven organization
Examples that demonstrate fundamental skills • Decoding words • Playing a scale in music • Hitting a backhand stroke in tennis • Being fluent with multiplication tables • Knowing basic procedures in science lab *Examples that demonstrate knowledge retention* • Knowing the parts of a cell • Understanding the rules of a game • Being aware of major legislation/public policy for a given historical period	*Examples* • Applying math problems (e.g., analyzing, predicting, justifying) • Creating a travel brochure to highlight features of a place • Scrimmaging before a game • Holding situational conversations in world languages • Writing a persuasive letter on an issue using a standardized format • Answering document-based questions • Doing a dress rehearsal for a performance	*Examples* • Interviewing community helpers to find out what they do and how they hope to affect others • Making a proposal to the principal concerning traffic flow or the time allotted between classes • Creating a podcast channel featuring interviews with members of the community on key political issues • Leading a local campaign on carbon emissions working with TakingItGlobal • Developing a plot map and the opening chapter of a story • Turning a school map into a friendly audio guide to help newcomers navigate the building

(just as a coach might during a sports scrimmage) and intervenes to provide insight and suggest potential actions. Rehearsals or scrimmages are crucial opportunities for students to pull together what they're learning and monitor their progress. When we increase meaningful rehearsal experiences, we're planting the seeds for fruitful authentic assessment opportunities.

As well as a rehearsal or scrimmage may have gone, we don't really know if the learner is an actual "player" until they have an **authentic opportunity** in a genuine situation with a genuine audience to independently be a player, a performer, an author, a scientist, or a historian. An authentic test demands application, sense making, feedback, and revision. It benefits from a clear purpose and target audience. It also depends on other forms of assessment to make students feel that what they're being asked to do is challenging, possible, and worthy of the attempt. It's not necessary to have frequent authentic assessments, but learners do need them from time to time; otherwise, they can get mired in drills and practice. Such assessments provide purpose, motivation, and an opportunity to gain confidence.

The three tiers of assessment are not an either/or moment. Students must engage in each of the tiers at various times. For example, if a learner is preparing for a tennis match, they may need significant practice on their backhand stroke or with their lateral movements. If they're preparing for the release of a podcast, they may need to become more skillful at using editing tools in a software platform such as Garage Band. If they're preparing for a cultural immersion experience, they need to engage in situational conversations in the targeted language and learn more about the customs of the region or neighborhood.

How to Develop an Authentic Assessment

This episode focuses exclusively on the third column—authentic assessments, such as a game or performance. We're not suggesting that you add on to an already overburdened assessment schedule. Streamlining has been one of our drumbeats, and it continues to apply now. As you survey your initial curriculum narrative, look for a handful of opportunities that are *compelling* and *worthy* enough for you to slow down and design an authentic assessment.

But what *is* compelling and worthy? From a teacher's point of view, some topics clearly lend themselves to authentic application. Or perhaps you base many of your units on a consistent set of priority standards. From a student's point of view, *compelling* and *worthy* may mean that they're doing complex, interesting, and important work, that assessments both motivate and measure their learning. The ultimate deliverable may be less compelling than the process and self-discovery along the way.

Four criteria are fundamental for an authentic assessment to be compelling and worthy from a student perspective:

1. **The assessment provides a real opportunity for students to solve an actual problem.** Students need to dive into a problem or explore an idea that has merit and purpose.
2. **The assessment is anchored in a specific place and context.** The situation is real, as opposed to simulated. The context can also change. An authentic learning experience might begin on the personal or local level and then expand to a global level. Conversely, a project with a global focus might eventually zoom in and become a highly personal one.
3. **The assessment involves an authentic audience.** The learning opportunity targets a specific audience whose members will provide feedback to the student. It could be an audience for a performance, users of a product or design, an expert panel, or readers of a publication.
4. **The assessment involves a realistic time frame.** This is necessary to provide a meaningful experience for the learner. In authentic demonstrations, students must work within time constraints and monitor their progress, which is a significant part of the learning experience. There's also the real possibility that students might engage in a long-term, multiyear authentic performance.

All four criteria are essential in developing learner roles and real-world competence. However, here we will focus on the second and third ones: anchoring the assessment in a place-based context and creating a deliverable for a target audience.

Learner Roles at the Core

As we develop storyboards and narratives that engage, we go back to our initial premise—that we fulfill the promise of the learner's role.

Figure 7. 2 is an early childhood storyboard illustrating the explicit connections to learner roles that students are assuming as they investigate, create, and share. Notice the great care the designer took in providing a preview of the quests to get

FIGURE 7.2

Curriculum Storyboard: Early Childhood Science

Early Childhood Science

Essential Question(s): **How do my senses help me explore what's in the natural world?**

Our year of discovery will ignite our curiosity and connect us to the natural world. We will record our discoveries in our adventure journals and add to our nature collections. We will learn to think like a scientist and connect with the natural world... one quest at a time! We will complete specific missions by going on wild, outdoor adventures. The adventures will involve all sorts of exciting, hands-on activities.

UNIT 1

What's around me? ↺

Using touch & taste to explore the natural world around me.

THE FOCUS OF THE STORY

We will start our year by exploring what's around us. We'll focus on using our senses of touch and taste.

AUTHENTIC DEMONSTRATION OF LEARNING

During our nature walks, we will gather seeds and experiment how they move when we drop them. We will adopt a very special tree to study and observe yearlong. We will look for signs of autumn, including fallen leaves, clusters of berries, and migrating birds. We will sketch these finds in our nature journals, paint a picture of autumn, and compare the colors we can find in our natural world. Lastly, we will look closely for fungus and mushrooms and wonder about the role they play in nature's recycling.

UNIT 2

What's Up? ↑

Using sight and hearing to explore the plants, animals, and sky above me.

THE FOCUS OF THE STORY

We then will look up and explore what's above us. We'll focus on using our senses of sight and hearing.

AUTHENTIC DEMONSTRATION OF LEARNING

We will observe how our feathered friends adapt to keep themselves warm as the weather gets colder. Next, we will do bark rubbings with crayon and include these in our nature journals. Lastly, we will experience the winter sky and weather and record what we see. During our nature walks, we will observe the cycles of the moon.

UNIT 3

What's down? ↓

Using smell to explore soil and water that makes life grow beneath my feet.

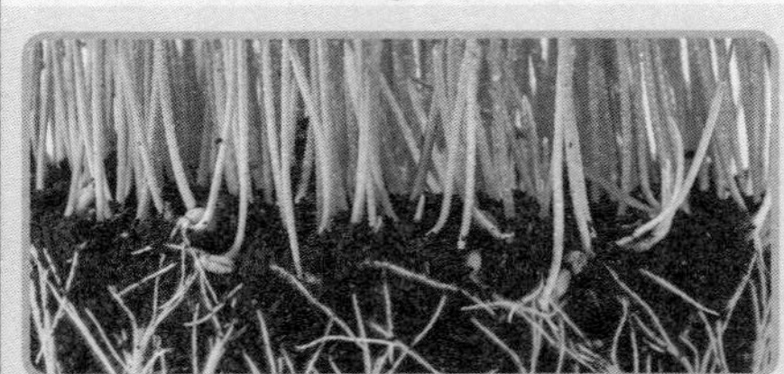

THE FOCUS OF THE STORY

Finally, we will look down and discover what's below us. We'll focus on using our sense of smell.

AUTHENTIC DEMONSTRATION OF LEARNING

We will observe how earthworms dig and eat soil along with decaying leaves and plants. We will sketch birds as they build their nests, hunt for garden snails, and notice how our special tree will look different now that it's bursting with life! We will sketch buds as they bloom and take a grass walk. Lastly, we will spot trees and shrubs in blossom and discuss the glorious scents of our favorite blossoms!

Source: St. Stephen's and St. Agnes School, Alexandria, Virginia. Used with permission.

students buzzing about these opportunities. You can close your eyes and imagine yourself as a young child listening to this story being read aloud. The simplicity of the questions, use of images, and sensory descriptions of the language combine to generate anticipation and energy.

When a student assumes a particular role for the authentic assessment—as a botanist, an architect, a community organizer, or an activities director—they're exploring the skills needed to develop their design and share it with a target audience. The deliverable should match the learner roles. For example,

- A *botanist* might produce a guidebook for visitors to a local park to document plants in a particular place or forecast the endangerment of a given plant species.
- An *architect* might produce a design pitch for a new structure or develop a prototype to illustrate the use of new technologies and materials for a prospective client.
- A *community organizer* might develop a petition for a cause or record a speech that encourages people to take action on an urgent issue.
- An *activities director* might conduct a needs and preferences assessment or develop a fitness program that encompasses a variety of skill levels and areas of interests for elementary school families.

Studying a variety of authentic examples will help students come up with ideas as to how they want to shape both content and form. Is this something a chef would do? How might a journalist approach this? What does a podcaster do once the raw footage has been recorded? What forms do their products, performances, prototypes, or solutions take? For example,

- For *botanists,* the **content** would include the plants to research and feature; the **form** might refer to a guidebook (its key parts, who it's for, and possible ways of organizing it).
- For *architects,* the **content** would include measurements and materials; the **form** would be building a 3-D model to illustrate the vision.
- For *community organizers,* the **content** might be a given cause; the **form** might be recording a speech that encourages people to take action.
- For *activities directors,* the **content** would involve assessing the needs and preferences of a target audience; the **form** might be developing a fitness program that encompasses a variety of skill levels and areas of interest.

The point is that this work is designed to affect a broader audience; it has impact beyond school walls. Students can show how the final product demonstrates their development of modern learner roles as part of a broader portfolio collection. Teachers can examine the products in light of suggesting additional refinements, as well as collect outstanding student models as sources of inspiration.

EXAMINE

When developing authentic assessments, the standards section of a curriculum document is usually a rich vein to mine. Note, though, that some standards focus on the practice and processes of a discipline, whereas others focus on content areas or domains; these different types of standards are more or less suited to particular assessment tiers. For example, relevant standards for *drill and practice* are often drawn from content standards that focus on discrete topics and skills. But relevant standards for *scrimmage or rehearsal* and *game and performance*—when students are actually "doing the discipline"—are drawn from those that describe applying learning to novel situations. Take a look at the high school Geometry storyboard in Figure 7.3 to see how the learning targets and divisionwide goals inspired the focus of the story and authentic applications.

Let's look now at authentic assessments in relation to a curriculum narrative and learning targets. As you read, try to identify ideas you might incorporate into your own curriculum storyboards.

- Develop possible solutions to produce 100 percent drinkable water that is free from any contaminants that may cause problems to public health, social life, sustainability, and the economy. **Possible learning targets:** *I can collect and analyze water samples to look for pollutants; I can design and test an idea to see if it mitigates damage from typical pollutants (such as irrigation pollutants, fertilizers, pesticides, chemicals, and industrial wastes)* [STEM Egypt, n.d.]
- Develop and present a stump speech (see Kavanagh & Ojalgo, 2012) to make a persuasive appeal to an audience on a teacher-selected or self-generated topic. **Possible learning targets:** *I can gather valid and relevant research on my topic; I can use details and emotions in my speech to inspire action.*

FIGURE 7.3

Curriculum Storyboard: Geometry

Geometry

Essential Question(s)
How do I become a mathematical problem solver to better understand the world around me?
In what ways can I communicate and represent my mathematical thinking?

Foundational Topics

THE FOCUS OF THE STORY

How do we classify and quantify geometric figures? We start our year using a pencil, straightedge, and compass to create lines and geometric shapes. We also learn the logical framework to use geometric properties to justify arguments.

TRANSFER GOALS

Analyze: Investigate, formulate, and construct viable arguments by taking risks, persevering, and thinking flexibly.

LEARNING TARGETS

- I can utilize logic to construct and judge the validity of a logical argument.
- I can analyze and construct basic geometric figures.
- I can utilize transformations to alter a shape's locations and orientation.
- I can solve problems involving parallel lines.

Triangles

THE FOCUS OF THE STORY

How do triangles and their properties form the fundamental building blocks of the physical world around us? Next, we discover new properties by constructing and comparing triangles using the foundational topics. We then apply the new properties to solve authentic applications such as GPS and Land Surveys.

TRANSFER GOALS

Explain: Communicate mathematical thinking by justifying solutions using multiple representations while attending to precision.

LEARNING TARGETS

- I can solve problems involving triangles utilizing their properties.
- I can prove triangles congruent and similar.
- I can utilize my knowledge of the Pythagorean theorem and trigonometry to solve real-world problems.

Polygons & Circles

THE FOCUS OF THE STORY

How do we leverage our knowledge of triangles to extend our understanding to more complex shapes? Next, we quantify and visualize real world phenomena such as earthquakes and sea level change. We utilize our understanding of geometry to better understand the phenomena by making predictions or drawing conclusions.

TRANSFER GOALS

Explore: Make sense of the world mathematically by asking questions and making connections through inquiry.

LEARNING TARGETS

- I can differentiate between the types of quadrilaterals and apply their properties to solve real-world problems.
- I can utilize properties of polygons to solve problems.
- I can analyze and apply circle properties to better understand the world around me.

3D Figures

THE FOCUS OF THE STORY

What new discoveries and understandings are required to better quantify the world in three dimensions? Lastly, we dive into the different 3-D shapes in order to analyze and apply their properties to practical situations.

TRANSFER GOALS

Apply: Utilize effective strategies, processes, and tools to model new situations and/or real-world experiences.

LEARNING TARGETS

- I can solve practical problems involving surface area and volume.
- I can apply concepts of similarity to three-dimensional figures.

Source: Virginia Beach City Public Schools, Virginia Beach, Virginia. Used with permission.

- Write a children's story (for example, a picture book, an early reader, or a fairy tale) to help make sense of an issue in your community. Issues for early elementary learners might include what friends do and don't do, what *equal* means, or how people treat you in a new place. Or they might involve more contemporary and complex issues. **Possible learning targets:** *I can identify information for my topic; I can organize my story in a sequence (that is, with a beginning, a middle, and an end); I can include details in my writing and illustrations; I can practice my story out loud to see where I can improve it.*
- Propose an appropriate menu (for example, suitable for low-sodium or dairy-free diets) designed for a particular audience, given health or medical concerns. Cook one of the dishes, and get feedback from your target audience. **Possible learning targets:** *I can research recommended diet restrictions based on a health or medical concern; I can identify recipes that appeal to my target audience; I can write clear descriptions of my menu items.*

Take a moment to review the ideas you've generated for your storyboard so far. Where within your narrative might it be worthwhile to slow down so that students can pursue an authentic challenge? What authentic formats come to mind for the genre setting you've selected? What related content and process learning standards and targets would bolster the significance of the exploration?

ACT

Here are some tips to consider when designing authentic assessments:

Focus on what matters most.

Survey your curriculum storyboard and identify possible points in the learning journey that are *compelling and worthy* enough to slow down to design a challenge. Consider the following:

- Does this topic generate lots of student interest?
- Which key learning targets in the course would benefit from an authentic application?

- Does the complexity of the topic warrant multiple viewpoints?
- Is the topic important and relevant enough that students will persist in the work?
- Does the challenge respond to a need? Does it have a clear purpose and deadline? Consider the best possible place for the demonstration of learning, rather than just putting it at the end of the unit or grading period.

Use realism to increase engagement.

Identify where the authentic experience will occur, and then craft an engaging and realistic scenario. The place should ignite fascination, curiosity, compassion, or outrage. For example, when high school students in a California school district were directly dealing with the impact of wildfires in their county, they were particularly motivated to determine prevention approaches and evacuation policies. Generally speaking, emotion is a great way to draw students in as responsive collaborators, adaptive problem solvers, and compassionate listeners. A detailed description of the place where the investigation and actions are occurring is central to inform student choices as they move forward in their quest. Place reflects the culture, climate, people, geographic features, and time of any phenomena. The study of place "keeps it real" for students.

Tap into students' creative powers.

For maximum engagement, ask students to probe the parameters of the authentic problem or challenge by incorporating questions like these:

- What might happen if . . . ?
- Is this true in all cases?
- What are the possibilities?
- What are the challenges?
- What solutions do you see now?

Offer multiple ways to demonstrate learning.

Generate an array of possible deliverables and demonstrations beyond the obvious to increase students' chances of being authentically engaged. Consider the following questions:

- What do professionals involved in comparable problems produce?
- What natural outcomes, services, products, and performances might result from your query?

Figure 7.4 presents a curated collection of authentic forms of assessment, organized by category. It's by no means complete, but it should help to spark ideas of your own.

Taking such considerations into account can broaden the assessment's relevance, meaning, and complexity. In deciding which of several possible inquiries to engage in, which formats to use to demonstrate learning, which resources they may need,

FIGURE 7.4

Authentic Forms of Assessment by Category

PERFORMANCES	SERVICES	REFLECTIONS
• Recorded and edited performance • Live performance • Design pitch • Game play • Storytelling • Poetry slam • Comedy routine	• Response plan to a specific individual's or family's needs • Participation in a global/local organization • Ambassadorship • Mentorship • Docent service for a museum or an exhibit	• Memoir • Observations as a journalist • Observations as a scientist • Satire • Sketch-noting • Portfolio • Log
ENTREPRENEURIAL OPPORTUNITIES	**VISUAL MEDIA FORMATS**	**PROTOTYPE PRODUCTS**
• Self-published book • Monetized video product • Business plan • App creation and publishing • Community service	• Documentaries • Trailers • Animation shorts • Animation narratives • TED Talks • Videos with digital effects	• Infographics • Blueprints • 3-D renderings • Interactive simulations • Design solutions • Catalog development
COMPOSITIONAL ACTIONS	**DISCOURSE FORMATS**	**MEDIA FORMATS (Audio only)**
• Mashing/remixing • Choreographing dance • Curated collections • Virtual museum • Interactive timeline • Cultural event or themed performance	• Global forum • Local issues forum • Simulations • Socratic seminar • Spider Web discussion • Reddit topic • Twitter chat with hashtag • Audio commentary • Website forum	• Podcast on an issue • Podcast series • Podcast narrative • Podcast interview • Music: Playlist sharing • Music: SoundCloud publishing • Music: iTunes publishing

and which checkpoints they must establish to monitor and share their progress, students function as co-creators of their experience.

In Our Next Episode . . .

Having explored key choices—setting, genre selection, and authentic assessment—we can now move forward with the curriculum storyboard's layout and design. The next episode clarifies how to make compositional choices and put the pieces together to provide a bird's-eye view of learning for students.

Episode 8

Generating a Curriculum Storyboard

Learning Target	Engage	Examine	Act
We can draft a storyboard narrative for a course using compositional choices to ensure learner engagement.	Explore elements and tips that will help in drafting an engaging storyboard.	Peruse examples of storyboards to consider which elements to include and to aid in drafting a course narrative.	Draft a storyboard narrative for a course using compositional choices.

ENGAGE

Thus far, we have set the stage for pulling elements together to compose a curriculum storyboard of a course across a school year. Looking back over our previous episodes prepares us to draft the storyboard. Let's take a look at the highlights.

Reviewing Previous Episodes

- **Episode 1** made the case for streamlining the curriculum in terms of both form and functionality, given the demands of cumbersome templates and overpacked, dated content.
- **Episode 2** focused on articulating vital modern roles for learners and using these as the means to reimagine their engagement with curriculum.
- **Episode 3** raised the necessity of taking an editorial stance to consider what to cut out, cut back, consolidate, and create when making choices for the curriculum narrative.
- **Episode 4** used brain-based research to clarify how human beings are wired for stories and make the case for formatting curriculum as a storyline as an effective way to engage learners.
- **Episode 5** described three settings for a curriculum narrative—disciplinary, interdisciplinary, and phenomena based—each of which can provide a fresh approach to content.
- **Episode 6** outlined five genres—based on topics, themes, issues, problems, and case studies—that can create rigorous ways to reimagine key content in a way that will engage learners.
- **Episode 7** dove into the importance of embedding authentic assessments in the storyboard as evidence of a learning journey across the school year and what constitutes a quality demonstration.

In this episode, we put these pieces together to lay out a process for creating a curriculum storyboard. We will work through drafting storyboard elements and storyboarding both horizontally and vertically before wrapping up with a set of tips for carrying out the process.

Drafting the Storyboard Elements

Most of us are accustomed to laying out the units across the school year in a fashion that makes sense to us as adults who have perhaps taught the same course for years. An assumption is worth challenging here, that *the connections among units* are evident to the learners. In fact, that's likely *not* the case, especially if they haven't studied the content before and are juggling multiple subjects and storylines daily. When we don't purposefully make those connections, it's analogous to an author writing a chapter book who has made no connections among the chapters and is just hoping the reader will find them.

For a curriculum to be a narrative, *the connections in the storyline must be explicit.* The curriculum storyboard helps students navigate connections across the important parts—the essential topics, issues, and concepts they need to learn, as well as the skills they need to develop. To achieve this continuity, teachers need to make deliberate choices for each unit regarding genre, setting, learning targets, and assessments. For example, a science teacher might explain to students that the first unit launches with the exploration of a problem and that the second unit highlights a case study that shows how a given solution to that problem emerged and played out. When you lay out the important parts in this way, you can see where to amplify, reorder, cut, or reframe to best engage your learners.

EXAMINE

The key to storyboarding a curriculum is creating a natural flow to the narrative across the school year, one that the learner can make sense of. Let's look at this more in depth with two school examples—one from high school Spanish and another from elementary reading.

Storyboarding the Narrative Both Vertically and Across the Year

As we begin to put the parts of the storyboard together, we want to show the power of what one individual design team can do in storyboarding a course as it connects to a vertically articulated curricular narrative.

- The title reflects the choice of **setting:** disciplinary, interdisciplinary, or phenomena based.
- The course or unit titles reflect an array of **genres;** they are based on topics, themes, case studies, issues, and problems.
- The images provide a focus and an **accessible cue for the learner.**
- The language in the narrative is **student friendly.**
- **Authentic assessments** offer opportunities to show a preview of what's to come.

Creating a storyboard conveys curriculum with a fresh lens for students—and that's exciting. And it's exactly the word *exciting* that describes the high school curriculum shown in Figure 8.1: a four-year scope and sequence for Spanish, crafted by Olivia Grugan, a world language specialist at the Appalachia Intermediate Unit 8 in Altoona, Pennsylvania.

Notice the deliberate connections and compelling iconography that Grugan made across years. She then developed course-level storyboards. Survival Spanish (see Figure 8.2) intrigues students from the start (Get in the Mindset), then has them consider how to make the most of their background knowledge (Take Inventory). Students see that the next steps on their journey will be learning to describe their basic needs (Locate Water) and familiarizing themselves with foundational vocabulary (Build a Fire), as well as using their Spanish in real-life situations (Start Signaling). Finally, the last column has students consider what's next (Keep Believing): now that they've come so far, will they continue their language-learning journey? Notice how language hooks students' imaginations, how it puts students at the heart of the journey.

Now let's look at a second example, from Waterford (Connecticut) Public Schools, which set out to develop a K–5 reading curriculum based on the science of reading. A vertical alignment team with representatives from each grade level, reading interventionists, literacy-focused instructional coaches, and administrators was assembled. Through collaboration, they articulated transfer goals based on the Connecticut Common Core State Standards and aligned with their district's "Vision of the Graduate." Next, they laid out existing unit topics and resources at each grade level to begin to uncover possible themes (see Figure 8.3).

Waterford literacy instructional coaches Deryn Winthrop and Kim Podeszwa shared these thoughts on the experience:

FIGURE 8.1

Four-Year Scope and Sequence: High School Spanish

Spanish 4-Year Narrative Map

Essential Question(s) **What is the "story of Spanish"?**

As you study the Spanish language and cultures over four years, you will move from surviving to thriving (survivor to thriver!). In the first year, you will use any tools available just to get by. The second year, you will acquire enough skills to navigate novel scenarios, enjoying exploration of a new place. In the third year, you will be able to appreciate the many facets of hispanic pop culture and some of their nuances. Finally, in the fourth year, your Spanish will have reached a level where you can actually discuss other subject areas with enough ease that you can study history, economics, politics and geography, all in the Spanish language. At that point, Spanish will have become the means by which you can enter new spaces, connect with new people, and explore any topic you choose. You will be thriving.

SPANISH 1

Survival Spanish

You will become: **A Survivalist**
flexible, persistent, humorous

You may never have spent the night in the woods, or built a fire from scratch, but you can be a survivalist too. Learning a new language is all about surviving (and eventually thriving!) in a new context. You did it once already , when you were a baby. You can do it again. Just like a wilderness survivalist, you will go through this year, step-by-step, acquiring your basic needs. By the end of the year, you will be able to enter any fully Spanish scenario and navigate your way through! Survival is not about perfection, but it is about success.

SPANISH 2

An Imaginary Trip Abroad

You will become: **A Traveler**
interdependent, risk-taker

You start this year with the basic skills needed to survive in Spanish. You are ready to travel. Pick a country and go through this year, imagining each part of your trip. You will start by preparing for the trip itself and getting there. Then, you will get to know a new city and settle in. You will explore, begin to establish a routine and decide how you want to spend your time. As you move to the end of the year, you will consider what life would be like if you stuck around for a bit. In this imaginative experience, you will acquire the skills necessary to travel to a Spanish-speaking place.

SPANISH 3

Hispanic Popular Culture

You will become: **An Influencer**
imaginative, open, delightful

Language is practical, but it is also beautiful. This year, you'll focus on the beauty of language. With the strong foundation you have developed over the past two years, you will explore different areas of popular hispanic culture. Start the year with music, a universal language. Then explore visual arts and the many colors of the Spanish-speaking world. Next, turn your attention to celebrities and style, then dancers and athletes. Finally, end the year with a healthy portion of yummy food. As you learn about each, you will dive deeper into the places and people that create these influences. You will even have opportunities to do some creating of your own.

SPANISH 4

How Spanish Spread(s)

You will become: **A Storyteller**
questioning, problem-solver

Spanish is the primary language in over 20 countries and is spoken by over 500 million people. But how did this happen? What historical, geographic, political, social and economic forces spread Spanish across the globe? This year, you will learn more about the history of the places where Spanish is spoken. Throughout this process, you will make connections to history topics you already know about and will learn about new ones you have never heard of. By the end, you will have a more global view of the 500 million+ who you are joining!

Source: World of Learning Institute Appalachian Intermediate 8. Used with permission.

FIGURE 8.2

Curriculum Storyboard: Survival Spanish

Spanish 1: Survival Spanish

People who survive in the wilderness or other dangerous situations have some traits in common. Survivalists have self-control, are adaptable, think outside the box and are resourceful. Survivalists even have fun. They know that staying positive and keeping their spirits up is half the challenge. They make mistakes, but don't let that crush them. They collaborate with others.

You may never have spent the night in the woods, or built a fire from scratch, but you can be a survivalist too. Learning a new language is all about surviving (and eventually thriving!) in a new context. You did it once already, when you were a baby. You can do it again. Just like a wilderness survivalist, you will go through this year, step-by-step, acquiring your basic needs. By the end of the year, you will be able to enter authentic, Spanish-language scenarios and navigate your way through! Survival is not about perfection; it is about success.

MODULE 1 **GET IN THE MINDSET**	MODULE 2 **TAKE INVENTORY**	MODULE 3 **LOCATE WATER**	MODULE 4 **BUILD A FIRE**	MODULE 5 **START SIGNALING**	MODULE 6 **KEEP BELIEVING**
 GET IN THE MINDSET	TAKE INVENTORY	LOCATE WATER	BUILD A FIRE	START SIGNALING	KEEP BELIEVING
FOCUS OF THE STORY	**FOCUS OF THE STORY**	**FOCUS OF THE STORY**	**FOCUS OF THE STORY**	**FOCUS OF THE STORY**	**FOCUS OF THE STORY**
The first step to surviving is to be in the right mindset. In this module, you will gain the basic tools and attitudes to learn a new language. These include a growth mindset, the willingness to make mistakes, and the willingness to take guesses! We will practice these.	Now, it's time to take inventory. What do you ALREADY have that will help you learn a new language and navigate a new culture? Some of these tools that you already have are words we use in English that are borrowed from Spanish, words that look similar in the two languages and context clues.	Before spending any more time, you'll need to locate water. All survivalists know that this is a basic need. In learning a new language, you also need to be able to access basic needs. In this module, you will learn to talk about food and water and where you are or want to go.	Fires are important for survival, but they are also a great place to connect with others. In this module, you will use the language you have learned so far to practice basic conversations that help you connect with new people and make friends.	With your whole camp set up now, it's time to try to communicate with the outside world. As a language learner, you are ready to venture into some unknown territory. This will be an opportunity to check out more real world language and see what you can understand. You will also learn about the many places Spanish is used!	By the time you get this far, you have successfully survived in a new language. But what's next? Survivalists plan for tomorrow. Are you interested in continuing your journey learning Spanish? What do you want to learn next? What skills do you hope to develop? Language learners believe in their future and that they can keep learning!

Source: World of Learning Institute Appalachian Intermediate 8. Used with permission.

FIGURE 8.3

Grades K–5 Scope and Sequence: Reading

K–5 Reading

KINDERGARTEN **Reading is My Superpower**	GRADE 1 **Reading is Thinking**	GRADE 2 **Readers Dive Deeper**	GRADE 3 **Reading is a Window to Our World**	GRADE 4 **Patterns and Change**	GRADE 5 **Peeling Back the Layers**
ESSENTIAL QUESTIONS	**ESSENTIAL QUESTIONS**	**ESSENTIAL QUESTIONS**	**ESSENTIAL QUESTIONS**	**ESSENTIAL QUESTIONS**	**ESSENTIAL QUESTIONS**
What do we read? Why do we read? How do we read?	What connections am I making? How do my connections turn into questions? How do I share my thinking about what I am reading? How do other readers affect what I think and wonder about?	How can I explore deeper with my reading?	Why do we read and how does what we read connect to our lives?	How does my prior knowledge and what I know about people shape how I read and respond to text? How do the stories people tell give insight into who they are?	How can exploring the perspectives of others help me to learn about myself?
SKILL FOCUS	**SKILL FOCUS**	**SKILL FOCUS**	**SKILL FOCUS**	**SKILL FOCUS**	**SKILL FOCUS**
Concepts of print Phonological & phonemic awareness Phonics Developing reading routines, habits, and stamina Comprehending and communicating about texts	Phonological & phonemic awareness Phonics & Word Recognition Developing reading routines, habits, and stamina Fluency Retelling with key details Describing characters Identify features of informational text	Phonological & phonemic awareness Phonics and word analysis Fluency Describe how characters solve problems Recount stories to ask and answer questions (who, what, where, when, why, and how) Determine central message, lesson or moral Use text features to locate information Identify topic and main idea	Phonics and word analysis Fluency Determine main idea and recount key details to support Describe character (traits, motivations, and feelings) and how their actions contribute to the sequence of events Determine central message, lesson or moral using key details Determine point of view(character/narrator/own)	Determine and interpret main ideas within a text based on key details and inferences Determine the theme/summarize a text, using details and examples from what the text says explicitly and when drawing inferences Describe a character in depth, using thoughts, words or actions Compare and contrast similar themes , topics and patterns of events in texts Analyze word choice	Determine and interpret main ideas within and across texts based on key details and inferences Compare and contrast similar themes, topics and patterns of events in texts Compare and contrast two or more characters using specific details related to how they interact Describe how point of view influences how events are described Analyze figurative language Determine the meaning of academic words or phrases

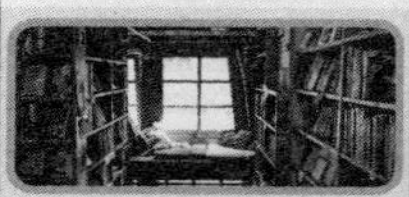

Source: Waterford Public Schools, Waterford, Connecticut. Used with permission.

> The process of storyboard development is powerful. At first, it was difficult to imagine one overarching question symbolizing an entire grade level's ELA curriculum journey. The gallery walk was critical in helping teams identify similarities and differences within their units. This resulted in compromise and intentional decision-making to reduce overlap, share priority skills, and scaffold grade-level instructional expectations. The best part, though, was being able to tell our "story" through visuals. (Personal communication, January 30, 2023)

Once they were clear as to their themes, questions, and primary skill focus, they began to draft curriculum storyboards back in their grade-level teams. Figure 8.4 illustrates the Grade 1 Reading draft in development. Note that it references both state-level reading standards as well as local school aspirations—both big-picture reading goals and the vision of a graduate.

Revising Drafts in the Storyboard Writing Process

Every curriculum writer we have worked with required several iterations to get to the storyline they liked; getting feedback and guidance was essential. Coaching tips in the ACT section of each episode can help with this task, along with a writing partner. Bena Kallick, an early supporter, coached several instructional leaders in fine-tuning their initial drafts. Here, she reflects on how curriculum writers can shift from "academic speak" when writing the focus of the story:

> When they see the power of the storyboard, they feel the burden of sounding authoritative is lifted, and they become jazzed. "This is a really great idea!" However, their first draft . . . [still reflects] their habit of stating objectives and outcomes. As a result, they might start their first draft . . . with a tone of, "first we will do this and then we will do this and at this point we will be doing. . . ." I have found these coaching questions help to shift the tone:
>
> - "Stop writing and just imagine a student from the past year. Maybe one that was having trouble feeling engaged. Keep that student in mind, and just talk to me. How would you describe your first unit so that it would be accessible and compelling to them?" As the coach, I capture some of what the person is saying in the template, replacing what they had and helping them shape it into the first story.

FIGURE 8.4

Grade 1 Reading

Grade 1: Reading

Essential Question(s) **What connections am I making? How do my connections turn into questions and predictions? How do I share my thinking about what I am reading? How do other readers' connections affect what I think and wonder about?**

Priority Reading Skills:
Phonics and Fluency: Phonological/Phonemic Awareness Skills, Phonics and Word Recognition, Fluency
Reading Habits: Developing reading routines and habits, stamina, building independence, partner work
Comprehending and Communicating About Text: Retelling, Character Traits, Theme - Text Features, Main Idea, Text Evidence

UNIT 1 | 11 WEEKS **Building Brain Power**	UNIT 2 | 8 WEEKS **Thinking About Characters and Their Feelings**	UNIT 3 | 6 WEEKS **Your Reading Journey So Far... What's Next?**	UNIT 4 | 8 WEEKS **Thinking About the World**
THE FOCUS OF THE STORY	**THE FOCUS OF THE STORY**	**THE FOCUS OF THE STORY**	**THE FOCUS OF THE STORY**
We start our year by building good reading habits and increasing our stamina. We develop strategies to decode words.	We continue our journey by going on adventures and exploring characters' feelings and lessons through poetry and stories.	We pause to reflect where we are in our reading journey and get ready to explore new strategies.	We end our journey by zooming in on nonfiction and exploring topics we want to learn more about.

BIG PICTURE GOALS

TRANSFER GOALS Students will independently...	**RELATED READING STANDARDS** From CT Framework	**VISION OF A GRADUATE** Waterford Public Schools
Apply the structure of language and text to decode and construct meaning. (4, 5, 10)	Anchor Standards: 4, 5, 10 Foundational Skills K-2: 1, 2, 3, 4	Communication, Critical Thinking, Self Direction
Read for pleasure, understanding, and knowledge to make sense of my world.	Anchor Standards 1, 4, 7, 9, 10	Research and Understanding, Critical Thinking
Lead reading experiences by making decisions about what, when, why, and how I read.	Anchor Standards 1, 10	Self Direction, Responsible Citizenship Communication

LEARNING TARGETS

PHONICS & FLUENCY	**READING HABITS**	**COMPREHENDING & COMMUNICATING ABOUT TEXT**
I will understand the basic features of print. (RF1.1)	I will build my reading stamina. (RF1.4)	I will identify key ideas and details in a text. (RI 1.1, RL1.1)
I will identify and change the sounds in words. (RF1.2)	I will make decisions about what, when, how, and why I read. (RF1.4)	I will retell a story (RL1.2)
I will break apart and blend sounds to read words. (RF1.3)		I will make predictions about a text. (RL1.7, RI 1.7)
I will use targeted strategies to read unfamiliar words and construct meaning. (RF1.3)		We will decide how to read and talk about a book together. (SL1.1)

Source: Waterford Public Schools, Waterford, Connecticut. Used with permission.

- "Now let's move to the next story. What do you hope the students will remember from the first story? What connections do you see to where you are heading? Why do you move from story one to story two? Tell me about your thinking." As the coach, I capture the thinking using their words as much as possible. I keep documenting the chart.
- By the time we are into the third story, the teacher is usually eager to just try it on their own and keep it moving. I step away and let them know that I can look at it again when they are done. (Personal communication, July 29, 2022)

Now it's time to consider some actions that teachers might take to translate their curriculum into a storyboard with their learners.

ACT

Knowing the elements in a curriculum storyboard is fundamental, but crafting a narrative is an act of thoughtful composition. Writers must make choices about how to deliver the story and reach the reader. Likewise, when teachers shape a curriculum, they need to make deliberate decisions to create a learning narrative that will touch the lives of learners.

Figure 8.5 identifies key curriculum storyboard components—title, image cue, focus of the story, and student connections—along with suggested coaching points. The examples shown come from a project that is being prototyped in Virginia Beach City Public Schools, with Allison as their thought partner.

Tips for Drafting the Storyboard Template

Translating the narrative into a storyboard template involves a set of practical choices. Here are some tips that can assist in the process.

Lay out the storyboard elements.

You should shape the storyboard to reflect what's most helpful for you in writing the narrative—and what's most responsive to your students. In Figure 8.1, the labeled rows reflect just that: the unit title and time frame, the image cue, the focus of the unit story, and the all-important space for students to reflect on the connection

FIGURE 8.5

Key Storyboard Components and Coaching Points

"Course Title"

Overarching Essential Questions to Frame Learning:

- Example in Algebra: How does modeling improve our ability to understand the world? In what ways can we represent mathematical ideas? What mathematical knowledge is necessary to understand linear and quadratic equations?
- Example in grade 11 English: How does American literature reflect and shape our concept of the American Dream? How do writers influence the reader with the choices they make?

Storyboard	Establish Criteria for Review	Conduct Review and Generate Possible Actions
Title	• Craft a title that is compelling and clear. • Select the type of unit focus that will best serve your purpose and engage your students (topic, theme, issue, problem, or case study).	• (Independent Living) Relationships: Family, Dating, and Parenting • (Grade 3 Music) It Takes Two to Make Some Har-Mon-Na-Ay! • (Grade 9 Health/Physical Education) It Does a Body Good: Exploring body mechanics with a variety of physical activity
Image Cue	• Select compelling images—photographs or icons—that help tell the story. Avoid generic clip art. • Consider what will motivate your learners. Include diverse images that reflect your learners, as well as authentic situations to explore.	• For a pre-K unit titled "Imagine It, Make It!" • For a grade 4 social studies unit titled "Wild Virginia"
Focus of the Story	• Write the focus as a narrative in an invitational style, using clear and accessible vocabulary for families and students. • Use purposeful transitions in telling the story to show the connections among units. Example: *—We start our journey . . .* *—Next, we explore . . .* • Develop a throughline that binds the story together and shows how the units within the storyline have a beginning, a middle, and an end.	• (Grade 3 Music): We begin by learning how to read new pitches based on the pentatonic scale, while expanding the range of our singing voices and exploring music from a variety of times and places. • (Grade 2 Reading): We deepen our understanding by drawing conclusions to help us determine the story's theme. Then we apply our knowledge of all our reading strategies to comprehend a variety of texts. • (Grade 4 Art): Art can challenge us to see things in a new way and can stretch our imagination. Discover how artists use innovative and repurposed materials in art. Artists often create unique works using exaggerated subject matter.
Student Connections to Storyline	• This blank space is for students to interact and tell the story. The students share their personal interpretation. The story becomes theirs. • Prompting questions help students draw connections, make predictions, and raise questions that they find compelling.	Sample prompting questions to launch connections: • *Patterns or connections between episodes I'm starting to see are . . .* • *Where I still feel lost is . . .* • *I wish we could spend more time exploring . . .*

among units. These labels are simple, efficient, and streamlined. However, there's always room for variation. For example,

- You might place essential questions under each unit title.
- Although you may wish to skip embedding images, we encourage you to include them. They focus attention, reinforce memory, engage the imagination, and reflect what's most compelling and relatable for the students in that setting. Students might suggest the image as well.
- You might prefer using bulleted points over synopses. Take into account the age of the learners. The key is for students to easily understand the text.

Agree on the storyboard components.

Consider what is essential to include in the 10,000-foot view of the course and then vet your ideas with teachers, students, and families. Throughout the book, you have seen different iterations of these high-level takes. For example, some schools ask for an engaging overview for the course, other schools prefer to use essential questions, and some schools actually prefer both.

Should the standards be referenced? What about authentic assessments? Should it include links for families to support learning at home? These are choices that are best made at a school or district level to promote clarity and consistency with students and families.

Compile your content.

Before creating the storyboard, consider the priority standards for your grade level or course. Look across your semester or yearlong set of units. What are the driving areas of focus? Using some of the ideas you have sketched out from thinking about setting (Episode 5) and genre (Episode 6), how might you reframe the perspective or approach to make it more engaging for your students?

Draw on what you know about your students.

Consider who your students are, what prior learning and life experience they may bring to the classroom, the resources you have available, and the demonstrations of learning you want students to engage in. They should see themselves in the story. This information should influence your search for images, the amount of text you draft, and the language you use. Ask yourself how you might adapt your story to *these students'* strengths and interests. How might you tell your story in a way that focuses their attention and invites them to engage with it?

Be a responsible storyteller.

Stories are powerful. As Neeley and colleagues (2020) explain,

> Stories can be used to comfort or confront, to clarify or complicate. They help audiences gain new perspectives and explore new knowledge. They help tellers gain greater insight into their own experiences and motivations, and to find purpose in their lives. Finally, storytelling is a key part of any collective change. (p. 4)

When crafting a curriculum narrative, always choose your content sources carefully, vet the information they provide, and keep an eye out for bias—both the sources' and your own. Sharing your efforts to carefully curate sources can support students' development as discerning, media-literate learners and well-informed citizens.

Keep it simple but avoid being simplistic.

Striking this balance is key, especially when designing on behalf of the learners. A key tip is to keep your sentences brief. Aim for phrasing that is concise, clear, and actionable.

Use vivid language.

As you're developing the storyboard, challenge yourself to use words, phrases, and photographs that will hook your students. Appeal to their senses. The more a storyline activates interest, emotion, and surprise, the more memorable it becomes.

Keep the narrative thread alive.

Make sure the title, image, and text all support one another. Use transition words to bolster connections for the students. Any misalignment can break the thread of the narrative. Does a compelling theme bind the unit together? How does it connect to previous and future units?

Streamline, streamline, streamline.

Part of the creative process is reworking and revising, which is necessary regardless of design expertise. Even though the process may feel frustrating at times, your end result will likely captivate the learners.

How does storyboarding curriculum impact learning? Mark Higgins, an 8th grade teacher and curriculum leader at Clark Lane Middle School in Waterford, Connecticut, shared these reflections with Allison:

> The old school approach to teaching social studies from when I was a kid was "Here are some facts." It wasn't cohesive, and it was easy to get lost and disengaged. Now, with storyboarded units, students can pick up the thread and make sense of it as they are moving through the experience. Middle school students thrive on structure and routine. Having a consistent theme throughout the course gives the course purpose, and it gives the students something they can hold on to, which in turn raises level of engagement.
>
> One of the hardest pieces for me was letting go of units or lessons that I was *very* attached to. While I miss them, I don't miss them that much because of the level of engagement I have now. I have never seen students so energized to talk about the content. And the growth the students are demonstrating is really remarkable.

In Our Next Episode . . .

The storyboard examples throughout this book focus on how to transform an existing course into one that's more engaging and accessible for students. In the next episode, we'll look at how you can boost learning at the student level through the development of reflective prompts, at the systems level through curriculum mapping and unit articulation, and at the planning level through learning sets.

Episode 9

Implementing Storyboards

Learning Target	Engage	Examine	Act
We can implement storyboarding by connecting with our learners, mapping within our system, and in daily planning.	Connect streamlining and using the storyboard approach with existing practices to amplify impact.	Examine storyboard implementation strategies via engaging instructional prompts, systemwide unit and mapping, and daily planning through learning sets.	Draft learning sets for specific learners, and streamline teacher planning time. Design prompts to encourage student interaction with storyboards and draft learning sets.

ENGAGE

Now that you have crafted a storyboard, how might you maximize its power in the lives of your learners? Let's circle back to the learning target in Episode 1—*We can evaluate the need for streamlining curriculum templates to increase their effectiveness and ease of use and better engage our learners*—to make sure that our creative efforts will have the desired effect on both the learning design and the learners themselves.

Generating a narrative thread is a worthy driver for students. As they encounter the curriculum, students explore the sequence units, move toward school expectations, and grow through authentic experiences.

This episode focuses on the effective implementation of storyboarding on three levels: instructional approaches with students, curricular approaches on a system level for unit design and mapping, and daily lesson planning in the classroom:

- **Student-level implementation** involves creating reflection opportunities for individual students to think about how *what* they're learning is affecting *how* they see themselves in the world and in the world of your classroom. The goal is to provide clear prompts that help students make their thinking visible, motivate their sense making, and stimulate conversation and analysis. It's important to avoid overly detailed and cumbersome directions or make classroom activities feel like "yet another thing" for everyone to do.
- **Systems-level implementation** involves using storyboarding to inform unit design and curriculum mapping in a variety of ways. We have seen firsthand how the narrative approach showcased in storyboarding can positively impact the quality of unit articulation and curriculum mapping within a school system.
- **Classroom-level implementation** involves the design of learning sets—a fresh take on daily planning. Learning sets employ the power of iconography and the consistency of clear prompts and student-facing language, offering a daily, granular-level parallel to storyboarding.

EXAMINE

What practices support the implementation of storyboarding on these three levels?

Starting with the Students

For learning to be significant, it must be reflected upon and recognized by students as something that is valuable to them.

We encourage a learning culture grounded in the shared belief that thinking is central to complex problem solving, rich collaboration, and the emergence of new ideas. The storyboard approach provides fertile ground to strengthen this kind of learning culture. There is such synergy between how we frame curricular content and how we cultivate dispositions in our learners (Kallick & Zmuda, 2017). How might we meaningfully connect the two such that students will interact with the narrative thread and discover more about themselves as they do?

First, let's take a look at some draft content for a 3rd grade social studies curriculum storyboard, developed by a group of teachers and administrators at Washington Episcopal School in Bethesda, Maryland (see Figure 9.1). Allison worked with Bena Kallick to generate some reflection prompts that were inspired by these educators' ideas. The prompts are posted in the row that follows the "Focus of the Story," as they are aligned to each quarter and grounded in the dispositions of *thinking about your thinking, applying past knowledge,* and *thinking interdependently.* (Visit www.habitsofmindinstitute.org to find more information on these dispositions and others.)

We also imagined several overarching questions to introduce at the beginning of the school year and revisit throughout—ones that would provide a big-picture view of the storyboard narrative:

- What are you discovering about yourself as a reader and creator of stories?
- In what ways did the story format shape your thinking about what makes a good story?
- Based on where we are in the story so far, what questions, connections, or new ideas do you have?

Asked again at the year's end, these questions can serve as an epilogue, a way to celebrate learners' journeys through storytelling formats, the knowledge they have gained, and the new ideas they have explored along the way.

As we reflected on these prompts—invitations to students to reflect and extend their thinking—Bena enchanted us by using the metaphor of planting a seed bed:

FIGURE 9.1

Curriculum Storyboard with Student Prompts: Grade 3 Social Studies

Grade 3 Social Studies

Esseintial Question(s) **Who am I? Who are you? Who are we? How does that shape and change the stories we tell?**

Overarching Themes: Identity, Community, Belonging, and Change

Social Studies Skills: Exploring value and accuracy of history, perspective-taking, "reading" historical texts from diverse formats, examining and reflecting on historical texts (e.g., audio, video, illustration, poem), developing stories in diverse formats

QUARTER 1
The Story in H*istory*

THE FOCUS OF THE STORY

Storytelling is how we learn about ourselves, others, and how we belong. This is the power of history — the stories that shape our collective memory and identity.

THE FOCUS OF THE STORY

You just finished writing a personal narrative. What did you hope someone would learn by reading this story about you? What did others learn about you from hearing your story?

Think about some keywords that describe you (ex. your personality, beliefs, interests). Write those words on a mind map graphic organizer. Look at similarities and differences. What connections are you seeing? What surprised you?

QUARTER 2
Listening to and Learning From Other People's Stories

THE FOCUS OF THE STORY

We explore cultures who have used or use oral storytelling to pass on their history, values, and traditions. Our focus will be Indigenous People and African-Americans pre-Civil War.

THE FOCUS OF THE STORY

You have read and listened to many stories from different cultures. What values and traditions do you see in these stories?

What are some of the values and traditions in a group you are a part of (such as extracurricular teams, family, class)? How would you describe the values and traditions of those groups to someone else?

QUARTER 3
A Picture is worth 1000 Words

THE FOCUS OF THE STORY

This quarter we look at visual art as a storytelling form. We explore a series of picture books, a global database with photographs, and murals in our local communities to better understand our communities.

THE FOCUS OF THE STORY

Telling stories through pictures, images, and illustrations is a powerful way to communicate.

Choose one of the most powerful images, pictures or illustrations. What made it so powerful for you?

QUARTER 4
Making Someone Else's Story Visible

THE FOCUS OF THE STORY

We end our year by researching someone else's story and capturing it using a format that you have explored at some point during the year. Make creative and responsible choices as you tell your story.

THE FOCUS OF THE STORY

You have studied different formats for telling stories — written, oral, and visual. Which format are you most drawn to as a reader and why? Which format are you most drawn to as a creator and why?

What have you learned about how stories shape and change the ways we think about people?

Source: Washington Episcopal School, Bethesda, Maryland. Used with permission.

> When you are starting the story, you are preparing the soil where students can cultivate ideas. They plant the seeds with their questions, connections to past knowledge, curiosities, and wonderments. They are embarking on either a continuing journey or starting new pathways. The storyboard becomes a garden in which those ideas can grow. The teacher provides the sun, the water, and the space for this garden of rich opportunities for learning. (Personal communication, January 20, 2022)

It may be helpful to print out the reflection questions so that students can paste them in their notebooks and interact with them easily on the page. Or you might provide a hyperlink that leads each student to a personal online space for prompts and reflections. Tools like a noticing notebook, quick video or audio recordings, or a box to collect intriguing ideas can also support students' reflections on learning experiences and question generation. The aim is to make it easy for students to capture and revisit their responses, draw on them during small-group conversations, compare inferences, make predictions, and generate new questions. And as you monitor or review these interactions, ideas, and questions, consider how these might drive new pathways that can be built into the current curriculum narrative or pursued through other learning opportunities. The "seeds" students articulate are the basis of Episode 11.

On to the Systems Level: Unit Planning and Mapping

Curriculum mapping, the careful laying out of curriculum and assessment across the school year and vertically from grades K–12, has a natural connection to a systems-level storyboard approach. Heidi, with her decades of work in this process (see, for example, Jacobs, 2004; Jacobs & Johnson, 2009), points out that teachers can easily transfer storyboards into mapping software as they lay out their academic year plans. When working on a curriculum mapping project with schools in the Archdiocese of St. Louis, she found that creating the storyboard and then moving it into curricular mapping software was not only easier than past mapping approaches but also produced stronger maps. Teachers found the "storyboarded-first" maps made more sense than those created directly in the software. As Beth Bartalotta, the principal of Saint Francis of Assisi School, shared with Heidi, "The storyboard makes the placement and alignment of standards natural for teachers. It also allows them to see how they are developing proficiencies across the school year" (Jacobs & Zmuda, 2023, p. 25).

On the unit planning level, the visual features of storyboards certainly attract student attention, but they also provide concrete clarification of the unit's conceptual focus, promising ideas, skill applications, and learning experiences. Recognizing that unit designs can prove helpful in planning *and* that they're often required, teachers can take elements from the storyboard and import them directly into a classical unit template design that is teacher facing in style and approach.

The contributions of Grant Wiggins and Jay McTighe (2005) to articulate units through a backwards design process have immense value, and we see storyboards as an asset in that endeavor:

- Stage 1: Identify Desired Results—*What are the goals for learning?*
- Stage 2: Determine Valid Evidence—*How will we know students have achieved the desired results? What do we accept as evidence of student understanding and proficiency?*
- Stage 3: Plan Learning Experiences and Instruction—*What will students need in order to perform effectively and achieve desired results? What activities will equip students with the necessary knowledge and skills? What will need to be taught and coached, and how should it best be taught in light of performance goals?* (pp. 18–19)

The systemic curriculum planning view reflected in mapping and unit design leads naturally to examining the daily planning work of the classroom teacher or teaching teams.

Working on the Classroom Level with Learning Sets

When teachers and students begin to experience a streamlined storyboard approach, with its keen sense of narrative and student-facing layout, old-style lesson planning can feel archaic. We recommend that the principles of storyboarding make their way directly to a streamlined, visually vibrant, and accessible planning approach, what we call *learning sets*. Think of them as lessons plans that are written as much for students and families as they are for teachers.

In the Prologue to this book, we mentioned the concern of a director for a magnet program in New Haven, Connecticut, whose schools were suddenly plunged into remote learning because of the pandemic. She wondered how schools could effectively communicate with students and their parents, given teachers' range of communication styles and the overwhelming number of tasks and activities in the curriculum. As she said to Heidi, "Our teachers are asking for a simplified curricular approach in *manageable chunks* for lesson planning." This request led to a prototype for lesson planning based on manageable chunks in a weekly format. It also called into question the language used in writing lesson plans, which wasn't user friendly at all. Teachers wrote those plans for themselves or for other teachers in purely teacher-facing language.

Thus, the initial move to distance learning clarified an essential truth—that our audience had changed. If students are truly stakeholders and partners in learning, *they* must be the audience for our learning designs. That meant figuring out how to best communicate with both students and parents and which actions and tasks would best support learning. We began to look at weekly lesson plans from the student's point of view, noting the need for easy-to-understand language, key prompts, and icons to guide action.

The Key Components of Learning Sets

Working with several districts, including Humble Independent School District in Kingwood, Texas, and Escondido High School District in Southern California, we developed a planning approach—learning sets—for communicating directly with students and their families. This approach streamlines both curriculum and lesson design.

Keeping true to our belief that visual communication is essential, consider Figure 9.2, which lists the key components of a learning set. Let's look at the components in more depth:

- **An easy-to-navigate template.** Format is central to streamlining—and this template is easy to follow.
- **Student-friendly language.** The learning set is written in language that is clear and accessible for students and their families.

FIGURE 9.2

Components of a Learning Set

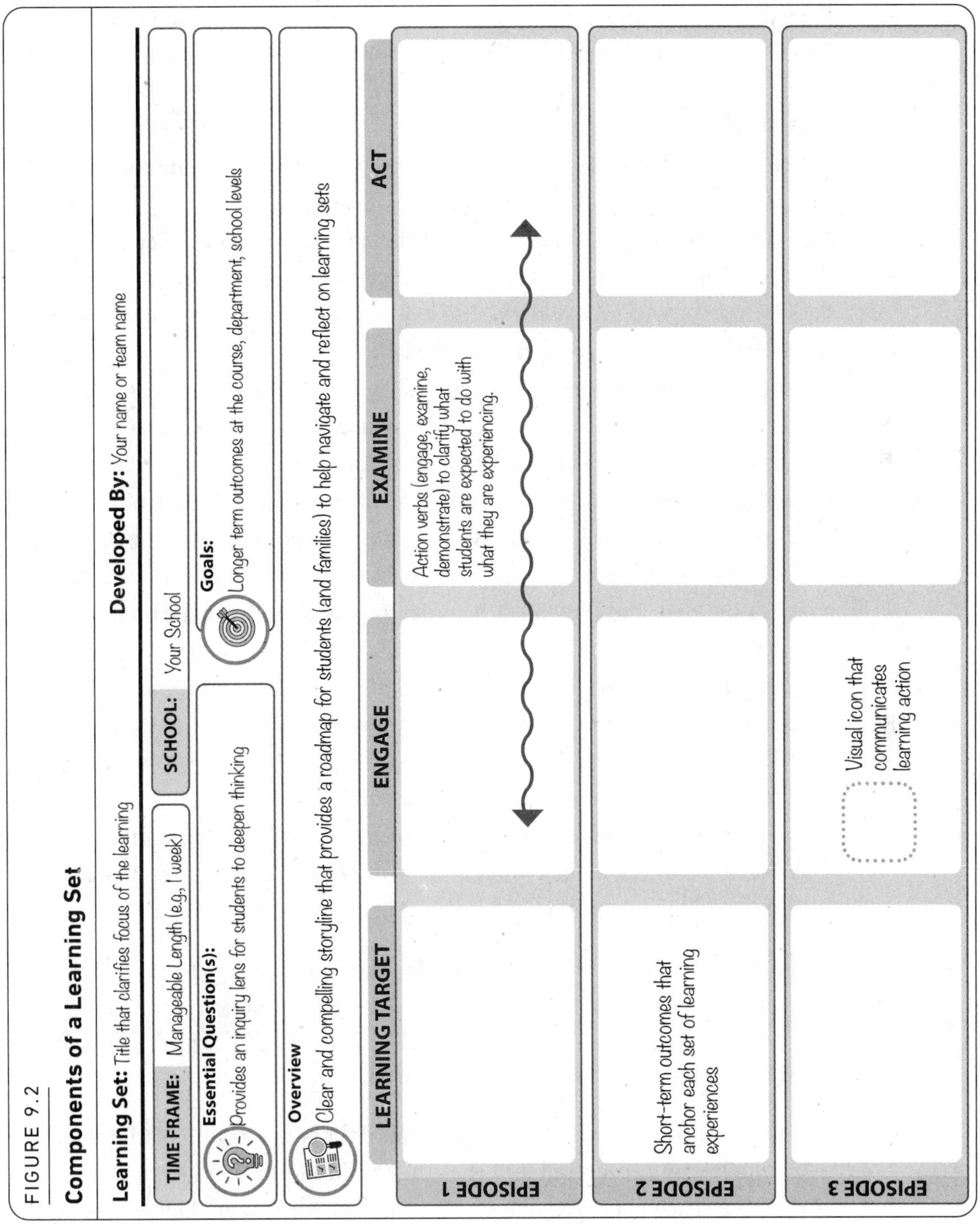

Learning Set: Title that clarifies focus of the learning
Developed By: Your name or team name

TIME FRAME: Manageable Length (e.g., 1 week)
SCHOOL: Your School

Essential Question(s):
Provides an inquiry lens for students to deepen thinking

Goals:
Longer term outcomes at the course, department, school levels

Overview
Clear and compelling storyline that provides a roadmap for students (and families) to help navigate and reflect on learning sets

	LEARNING TARGET	ENGAGE	EXAMINE	ACT
EPISODE 1			Action verbs (engage, examine, demonstrate) to clarify what students are expected to do with what they are experiencing.	
EPISODE 2	Short-term outcomes that anchor each set of learning experiences			
EPISODE 3		Visual icon that communicates learning action		

- **Goals.** Goals are connected to the relevant modern learner roles that students will assume within the learning set—for example, as scientists, historians, or researchers. Goals are also reflected in authentic assessments, both formative and summative.
- **Essential questions.** Cited in the overview, essential questions encourage focused inquiry. They also may apply across units and subjects.
- **The overview.** This provides a clear, brief, and compelling description at the top of the learning set. Although it may be tempting to pack in many details and goals in an overview, the key is to crystallize the point and to focus on the student as the reader of the set.
- **Episodes framed by learning targets.** The word *episode* denotes a natural sequence of events in a story. It's a playful and deliberate frame for the narrative that students are experiencing. Each episode commences with a student-facing learning target—a clear statement derived from standards or mission-driven goals of what a learner needs to know or be able to do. These targets are smaller, more manageable goals in service to the overarching goal, and they must be written in accessible, invitational, and actionable language (as "I can" statements).
- **Action verbs that engage learners.** The prompts motivate and direct students to *play out* the target through three verbs like *engage, examine,* and *act* (or *demonstrate*). These prompts require learning set writers to craft statements that are clear, concise, actionable, and expansive.
- **Iconography.** The human eye fixes on images much faster than on written text. Throughout this book, you've seen how we use icons to preview each episode. Here are some other examples of icons we've used in our work:

Analyze | Brainstorm | Design | Model | Perform

Yalanska (2016) notes that icons speed up data perception by enhancing the memorability of an element and that they facilitate navigation through a site or material. They also save space on a screen or page by replacing long words or phrases. Using icons has two benefits in this setting: first, there's less of a need for written text because students are visually cued to an action; second, teachers can quickly recognize patterns in their instructional practice and vary experiences to meet learner needs and refresh tired approaches. Designing icons with students to generate higher-level types of interactions can be an effective way of partnering with them in the planning process.

Now why should teachers and school leaders consider using learning sets? We've found that showing what the sets look like, explaining why they matter, and contrasting them with older-style approaches are quite effective as motivators. Figure 9.3 helps to clarify why traditional lesson plans tend to develop teacher dependence and learning sets tend to develop learner independence.

To make the comparison of the approaches even clearer, let's look at examples from a school group that field-tested learning sets.

FIGURE 9.3

Traditional Lesson Plans and Learning Sets: A Comparison

Traditional Lesson Plans	Learning Sets
Lists of directed tasks include assigned readings and steps for students to decipher.	The learning set has a clear format and is written in easy-to-follow sequences that are highlighted by icons.
Students are required to figure out assigned tasks that might not require a demonstration to show learning or engagement.	Action prompts are simply written and are accompanied by icons that lead to engagement.
Each teacher has their individual approach to lesson plans, so students must decipher varying directions from multiple teachers.	Consistent prompts from the teacher and a consistent template make this approach easy for students to use.
The lesson plans develop teacher dependence.	Learning sets develop learner independence.
Frequently occurring patterns and repetitive experiences characterize lesson plans.	Icons flag a variety of learning experiences, ensuring a greater variety of ways that students can demonstrate their learning.
Lesson plans do not necessarily link back to the overarching unit design.	Episodes directly connect to the overview, and all prompts connect to the learning targets in each episode.

From Old-Style Unit Design to Learning Sets

Having explored the reasons for learning sets and having seen some examples, a team of teacher leaders from Vista High School in California agreed to take on the challenge. The team's aim was to convert a traditional unit design and accompanying lesson plans into a streamlined learning set. We shared the icons, the learning set features, and the visual format to support their curriculum design. Figure 9.4 shows an excerpt from a Life Science course they created.

Because of the icons, the student can see at a glance what actions are called for; it's immediately apparent if a given activity offers only a single choice or just repeats a choice that the designer inadvertently may have overused or just automatically defaults to. Notice how the designers have expressed both the learning targets and the text in the columns titled Engage, Examine, and Demonstrate as "I can" statements. Notice also the consistent use of icons, which are paired with a verb that describes them, such as *watch, discuss, design,* and *present.*

Craig Gastauer, one of the teacher leaders at Vista High School, shared these thoughts on the difference between their old approach to curriculum design and this new one:

> When we have attempted to do curriculum design as a school, the overwhelming response from teachers has been that they spent hours, even days, creating these documents but were still no closer to having finished lessons, activities, or projects that would be used in the classroom. Most teachers believed that filling out unit planner templates was akin to jumping through hoops to satisfy a district or site mandate.
>
> When Heidi and Allison first shared learning sets with our group, I was both intrigued and excited—specifically about two ideas.
>
> First was the student-facing language. Teachers were more positive about creating a plan that clarified the "big picture" because the audience for it was *students.* It had us focusing our efforts to ensure we were helping students develop concepts and skills in alignment with the unit's overarching goals while chunking the learning into targets that were manageable for them. The learning set could also act as a road map for student success, as the "Engage," "Examine," and "Demonstrate" sections clearly connected their tasks and actions to the learning target they were expected to achieve.

FIGURE 9.4

Learning Set: Life Science

Learning Set: Fighting Off Infectious Disease **Developed By:** Craig Gastauer

TIME FRAME: 8 Days **SCHOOL:** Vista High School: Life Science

Essential Question(s): How do we get sick? What do our cells do to fight off infection? What behaviors might we adopt to protect ourselves from infectious disease?

Goals: Describe how the structures (of the endomembrane organelles) allow for the function of the body system (exocytosis of proteins). Communicate scientific information accurately and powerfully to varying audiences.

Overview: In these post-Covid times, it's important to understand how to communicate to others (teach) what they might be able to do to protect themselves to the best of their abilities based on an understanding of cells and human behavior. We will examine how the structures of cell organelles determine the functions a cell may carry out. We will also build upon the Habit of Mind: Thinking and Communicating with Clarity and Precision to explore how to best communicate scientific knowledge to a diverse audience with potential misunderstandings about the science and its potential agency and impact.

	LEARNING TARGET	ENGAGE	EXAMINE	DEMONSTRATE
EPISODE 1	I can describe the functions of the endomembrane system organelles.	After reflecting and discussing with partners about past learning of the cell, **draw and label** a representation of an animal cell. Include a quick blurb on what each cell structure does. 	**Collaborating** with your team, engage with the interactive cell presentation: - Identify what you remembered - Revise mistakes, incomplete info - Add new labels to cell structures / functions	**Analyze** your developing understanding of the endomembrane organelles of a cell and predict how they might work together to deliver a protein outside the cell.
EPISODE 2	I can create a plan to minimize my chances to be infected by a specific infectious disease.	**Watch** the YouTube video in Canvas with your table group using the "See - Think - Wonder" routine to explore Infectious Diseases.	**Investigate** one of the infectious diseases listed in Canvas (or propose your own) and determine: - How humans are infected - Symptoms of disease	**Design and present** a plan in the form of a video PSA (to employees at a part-time job, members of a church group, members of a sports team you interact with, etc.) to follow to minimize your chances of being infected by your selected infectious disease.
EPISODE 3	I can describe the roles of the endomembrane system organelles to fight off infectious diseases.	**Watch** the video showing the movement of proteins through the endomembrane system. **Make connections** between this 3D model of organelles with those in your drawing.	Prepare a jigsaw presentation by collaborating with your "Expert Group" to give to your "Home Group" using available digital and print resources.	**Create and present** a cell model to demonstrate an understanding of how cells transfer proteins to the bloodstream to fight off your identified infectious disease. **Create** an FAQ page based on the questions generated from this presentation. 

Source: Vista High School, Vista, California. Used with permission.

> The second thing that excited me was the visual layout of the document and the intent behind making it visual. The icons can help all students better understand what is expected of them and can help the teacher reflect on the varied use of pedagogies. Many students, specifically those who are English language learners or have an IEP, benefit from having supports to help them recognize what is expected of them. With the learning sets, language is still an essential component for students and recorded within the document. Teachers don't water down instructions or expectations. At the same time, each visual icon provides the student with the visual clue to make sense of the language that may still be difficult for them. (Personal communication, September 29, 2021)

As Craig notes, the deliberate and direct outreach to students through the design of learning sets is key to their effectiveness.

ACT

A curriculum narrative is successful when students can find and elaborate on connections among the units displayed on the storyboard and expressed in learning sets. As writers of curriculum, it's our job to position learners to interact with curricular content, generate evidence of their insights, and apply those insights to develop deeper and more nuanced understanding.

Eliciting Student Responses

How can we nudge learners to find connections among units and develop their own individual takes on the material? Through careful prompting that's built on questions like these:

- *In what ways do the essential questions guide your thinking?* Imagine a sophomore, driven by the essential question *What does dystopian literature reveal about our society?*, cataloging the ways in which *Brave New World* reminds her of today's influencer culture and its advocacy of finding happiness through consumption. After the English teacher prompts the class to apply this essential question to the works read earlier in the semester, the sophomore argues in an essay that because dystopian fiction permits the exploration of human society from perspectives that are not restricted by current political affiliations, "it can reveal a truth that is truer than what we read in news reports or realistic fiction."

- *As you read about the ideas, concepts, events, or people highlighted in a learning set, are you finding them again in other units? What does that suggest to you?* Imagine a 5th grader who is intrigued by the extraordinary distances birds travel across the world going on to track the migratory patterns of specific birds in his home area across the school year. Imagine a 9th grader studying World War II midway through a world history course thinking back to what she learned in September about the role of leaders throughout history and their impact on people's lives.
- *What skills are you developing as you move from one episode to the next?* Imagine an 8th grader who watches a video clip using Cloudapp in a learning set episode on immigration electing to develop her media-making expertise and use the app in an independent project. Or imagine a 2nd grader connecting the science unit on simple machines and how form follows function to a subsequent science unit focused on how animals adapt to their environment.
- *What are you uncovering about yourself as a learner along the way?* When learners become immersed in making connections and crafting ideas, they reveal themselves. This may be a powerful time to incorporate prompts that connect to Habits of Mind dispositions: thinking about your thinking (metacognition), thinking interdependently, and applying past knowledge. See Appendix D for an example Allison developed with Bena Kallick. You can also visit https://www.habitsofmindinstitute.org to learn more about the dispositions.

Periodically throughout the year, have students pause and reflect on the narrative thus far; have them also look ahead and predict future connections. They can see how the storyboard houses the learning sets and the power of daily experience. The link between the big picture and the activities are literally visualized. On all levels—the individual student level, the instructional level, and the school systemic view—connections are explicit and reinforced.

The Steps to Creating a Learning Set

Let's look more closely at steps you need to take to create a learning set for your students using your curriculum storyboard.

Step 1: Select the unit for the learning set.

Identify the title of the unit, time frame, and focus of the story which should be consistent with the curriculum storyboard. For details, see Episode 8.

Step 2: Write the overarching goals.

The learning goals should be purposeful, easy to understand, and free from educationese. Include a few meaningful goals rather than a long list that the student will likely ignore. They may come from "big picture" disciplinary goals or schoolwide goals. For details, see Episode 2.

Step 3: Determine essential questions.

Framing the learning set around one to three essential questions written in student-friendly language stimulates investigation and clarifies the focus. Such inquiries can launch initial investigations and guide students through deeper analysis, thoughtful conversations with peers, self-reflection, and self-discovery. For more details on how to draft essential questions, see Jay McTighe and Grant Wiggins's excellent book, *Essential Questions: Opening Doors to Understanding* (2013). Placing the essential questions in the overview signals their pervasiveness throughout the set of learning experiences. You can find examples of essential questions in Episodes 4, 6, and 8.

Step 4: Identify three action prompts.

This is crucial to the process. The Vista High School group chose to *engage, examine,* and *demonstrate.* Humble Independent School District in Texas used the prompts *explore, create,* and *share.*

Why three prompts? A set of three is manageable in a way that a long list is not. The prompts launch students into consideration of key ideas, concepts, and information; guide them into an examination of the ideas through inquiry; and then steer them directly into a demonstration of learning. The demonstration aligns directly to the learning target, stated goals, and essential questions.

Step 5: Enter learning targets.

Launch each episode and set of prompts with a carefully designed learning target. Learning targets are the translation of standards or objectives into student-friendly language. They usually commence with an "I can" statement to develop the targeted skill or proficiency. A learning target invites the student to reach the target through fulfilling the tasks and the actions directed in the three prompts. The fulfillment of the "I can" statement leads directly to evidence—that is, to an assessment.

Step 6: Describe related actions.

The first action (*engage* or *explore*) launches students into the narrative and typically provides context or background knowledge as they become immersed in the situation, problem, challenge, or case study. The second action (*examine* or *investigate*) prompts thoughtful analysis within and across texts, perspectives, or approaches. The final action (*demonstrate* or *act*) clarifies an assessment that provides evidence of the learning target. If you're developing this in Google Classroom or in a learner management system, provide hyperlinks to resources such as readings, assignments, and graphic organizers.

Step 7: Place icons.

The strategic placement of icons indicating the type of action required is both purposeful and playful. Students can see at a glance the array of experience types in which they will engage. In turn, the icons clarify for the teacher the range of instructional approaches offered. To promote student engagement, have students design icons for the learning sets.

Implications for Curriculum Mapping and Unit Design at the Systems Level

The learning set is a subset of the unit design and curriculum map, laid out in the storyboard to help ensure coherence and fidelity to both the standards and the school's broader aims. Aligning the learning set to the focus of the story, the essential questions, the learning targets and standards, and significant demonstrations of learning is central to the fulfillment of the narrative. On a daily basis, then, students experience their curriculum—whether it's Algebra I, Our Neighborhood, Rocks and Minerals, or any other course or unit—as an engaging exploration.

The design challenge is to encourage this exploration while keeping the flow of the narrative focused and clear to each learner.

In Our Next Episode . . .

We have now clarified how to transform existing topics into narratives through a course curriculum storyboard (Episode 8) and related learning sets while using instructional prompts to engage students in the learning experience (Episode 9). The next two episodes are dedicated to phenomena-based narratives—emergent problems, topics, and ideas that capture headlines, inspire action, and can have a significant effect locally, nationally, or globally. Because there's no "end" to the story (it's happening in real time), we introduce a new curriculum design organizer that will help you frame these narratives.

Episode 10

Framing Emergent Narratives

Learning Target	Engage	Examine	Act
We can pursue emergent narratives to keep curriculum vital and relevant.	Explore the origins and nature of emergent narratives and the use of the pitch-to-pitch model.	Analyze examples of teacher- and student-generated emergent narratives in curriculum.	Identify strategies and approaches to developing emergent learning opportunities.

Engage

No matter how compelling the curriculum narratives are, they still need room to breathe. How do we pump oxygen into the curriculum? By keeping space for unexpected diversions that make the journey come alive, for emergent local and global issues that are unanticipated, unpredictable, and sometimes unnerving. We reserve space for exploring and acting on ideas that we can curate, prototype, express, and share with the world. What energizes students and teachers are opportunities to make sense of thorny problems; develop an idea that provides relief, justice, or joy; and celebrate creative expression or our fascination with the universe. In the absence of such a space, our curriculum storyboards can become fortresses that shield students from the world. Any curriculum, no matter how engaging, becomes brittle when there's limited space for improvisation.

Creating an Emergent Narrative

Generating and developing an emergent narrative require a design model more akin to creative pursuit. The model needs to be flexible and malleable; it's not designed to have a permanent place in the curriculum. What sparks this creative pursuit is a connection to a problem, a challenge, an issue, or an idea. Action can begin by uncovering root causes or user concerns or by collecting and archiving snippets of inspiration to grow an idea.

Now, given the fact that an emergent narrative may be expendable—a "one and done" journey that you'll likely not repeat—you may be asking yourself why you'd put in the time, energy, and effort to design this way. Here are a few reasons:

- Emergent narratives put modern learner goals in the forefront.
- Emergent narratives model a process for engaging with problems, challenges, and issues that are complex, ambiguous, and sometimes volatile.
- Emergent narratives develop student capacity for engaging in independent projects within and beyond school walls.

Granted, it can feel like a jump to go from interests and fascination to active exploration. How can we help learners spark inquiry and craft ideas? What strategy might encourage them to generate, shape, and test drive possibilities?

The Power of a Pitch

The notion of *making a pitch* is fundamental in a variety of professions. The pitch launches a creative possibility for action. There's an energy and immediacy to throwing out an idea that, by nature, is phenomena based. It's emerging from the here and now, and we can't prescribe it.

The word *pitch* has multiple definitions; the third one in the *Merriam-Webster Dictionary* (n.d.) stands out: *Pitch: to present an idea for consideration.* Pitches are a crucial component in the fields of design, marketing, and film production. Someone presents a streamlined concept in the hope of getting the time and resources to construct, field-test, draft, or create a product, performance, or service. The presenter must show how the concept will affect the intended audience or receivers of the service. Making an efficient pitch requires sufficient knowledge to get the query started, a genuine commitment to the intended recipients, and a willingness to learn.

Here's how the *Harvard Business Review* (Quinn, 2020) describes a successful pitch:

> It is your empathy for your audience, your passion for meeting a challenge together with them, your ability to listen, speak directly, and apply your expertise in the pitch. It is also the tone you can create in the room—presenting yourselves as a club your audience wants to join, knowing how to surprise, delight, and engage your audience with your unique version of relevant expertise and problem-solving, live. (para. 16)

Providing an opportunity for students to create a pitch concurrently develops the requisite skills and confidence to discern, shape, and share authentic personal possibilities. Pitches are not contrived; there is no *snap! now it's time to be creative,* which you sometimes get with genius hour or capstone projects, as engaging as they might be. What we need is not a set block of "creativity time" on a Friday afternoon but to build into the ethos of the classroom the clear understanding that a student can *always* make a pitch for an investigation or a creative sketch—and, what's more, that we encourage it. The source can come from within the student's personal experience, a local endeavor, a point of fascination, a global problem, or an offshoot of the ongoing curriculum. The teacher will obviously not drop everything for a student to dive into a quest; what we're saying is that we need to make space in the curriculum for students to pursue what captivates them.

We designed the pitch-to-pitch model using an infinity sign to denote the unbounded and limitless nature of the exploration and design of an idea. As you can see in Figure 10.1, the process starts with a pitch, moves into the exploration and deliverable loops, and evolves into a revised pitch or a new pitch entirely.

Let's look at these elements more closely:

- The **pitch** shares the value of an exploration to galvanize interest and resources. The pitch is informed by genre selection (an issue, a problem, a case study, and so on); source (an idea, a question, or a challenge); and scale (the desired effect at a personal, local, national, regional, or global level).
- In the **investigation loop,** the student generates sketches with regular feedback. Sketching is a way to capture ideas—words, images, or both—to inform the ongoing exploration; it does not generate a formal or finished product.
- In the **deliverable loop,** the student designs a product, a performance, an experience, or a service with a target audience for a given purpose.

When reading the model from left to right, it may appear to be a process that moves cleanly from start (pitch development) to finish (product development). But as the arrows indicate, there's no definitive starting or ending point. In fact, one value of developing and sharing a product or creation is that it helps to clarify a revised

FIGURE 10.1

The Pitch-to-Pitch Model

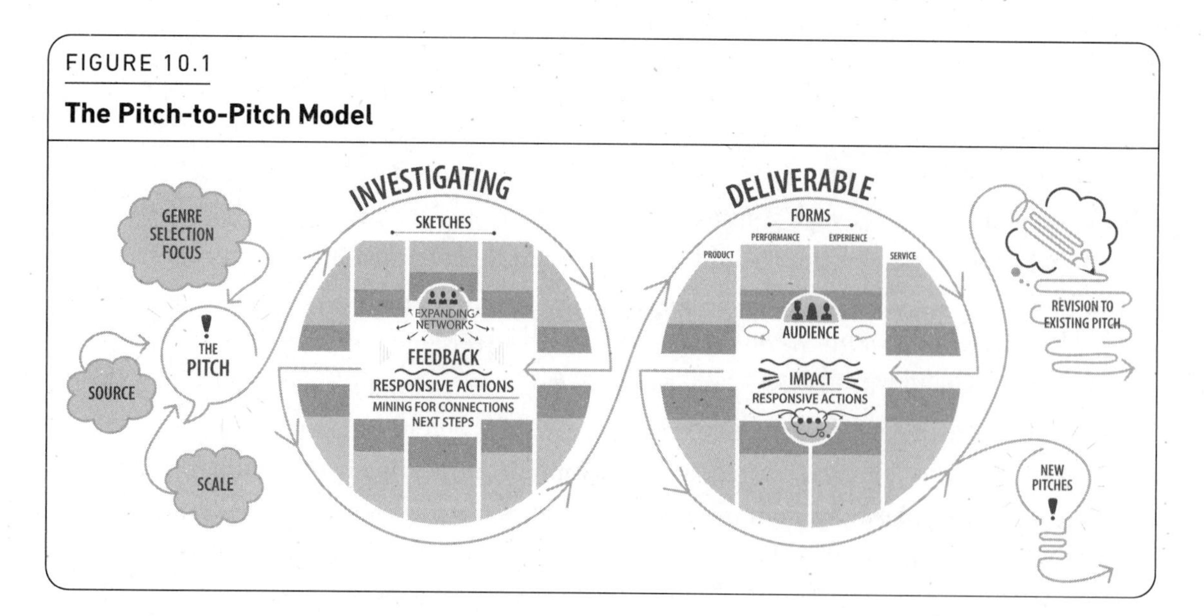

or new pitch. For example, examining an architectural model of a proposed sports stadium can inspire a student to try new things while creating her own model for a local sports center. These influences do not have to be deliberately consulted; many arise naturally while the student is exploring various products or creations. Sometimes teachers suggest possible deliverables (e.g., a screenplay, memoir, or podcast) to increase student understanding of how different communication forms capture pitch ideas.

Entry Points for a Pitch

An emergent narrative journey can start with *an immediately significant event or situation*—for example, the 2022 Russian invasion of Ukraine, the discovery of water on Mars, the birth of a new family member, or watching Lin-Manuel Miranda's musical *Hamilton* for the first time. These events can shift perspectives, raise questions, and generate new aspirations.

The narrative can also begin with *an emergent and compelling question*. For example, What is the cost of supporting vaccine efforts in low-income countries? How is climate change contributing to more frequent and widespread famine? What can we grow in our garden to improve our health? Why do some people not have homes?

A third entry point for the journey stems from *an ongoing collection and curation that captures fascination, curiosity, and wonderment*. In her book *The Creative Habit*, Twyla Tharp (2011) describes her creative process when she starts to develop choreography for a new show. She labels a box to collect and nurture ideas:

> That's how a box is like soil to me. It's basic, earthy, elemental. It's home. It's what I can always go back to when I need to regroup and keep my bearings. Knowing that the box is always there gives me the freedom to venture out, be bold, dare to fall flat on my face. Before you can think out of the box, you have to start with a box. (p. 88)

Tharp promotes having a place, such as a drawer, notebook, or folder, to house these ideas for regular reflection. She also recounts a story about Beethoven's process when developing a new piece of music:

> He would scribble his rough, unformed ideas in his pocket notebook and then leave them there, unused, in a state of suspension, but at least captured with pencil on paper. A few months later, in a bigger, more permanent notebook, you can find him picking up that idea again, but he's not just copying the musical idea

> into another book. You can see him developing it, tormenting it, improving it in the new notebook. . . . He never puts the ideas back exactly the same. He always moves them forward, and by doing so, he reenergizes them. (p. 83)

Having a place to put snippets of fascination and wonderment helps capture sparks of interest without worrying about what form they will ultimately take or without having to justify why they're interesting.

Regardless of the entry point, the pitch and investigation are designed to prompt ideas worth pursuing. They're "intriguing little tickles at the corners of your brain" (Tharp, 2011, p. 82) that will help shape the learner's journey—as well as become the spine for a deliverable.

EXAMINE

Children and young people are naturally curious, but curiosity, like all useful and creative habits, dissipates if it's not nurtured. If students are not able to routinely pursue right-now learning and interests in school, their ability and will to attend to possibility can dwindle. In place of the occasional token gesture for students to suddenly "get creative," we suggest the pitch model.

Perhaps you're thinking, "Yes, but can you show me what the pitch model looks like when it's employed in a school?" We're happy to do this. As you are reading through the experiences in this section, make a note of the ideas you find intriguing. What questions might you have in relation to the feasibility or appropriateness of these efforts in your own school?

The Quest Model at McGee Middle School

At McGee Middle School in Berlin, Connecticut, library media specialist Danielle Salina developed an award-winning program for 8th graders called Quest (see https://sites.google.com/berlinschools.org/mcgeelmc/quest). It's based on the Quest model featured in *Bold Moves for Schools: How We Create Remarkable Learning Environments* (Jacobs & Alcock, 2017). In McGee's program, each student develops an authentic query with a corresponding deliverable to provide a service or solve a problem that is both worthwhile and feasible; they must post their research plan, their deliverable plan, and their sharing-of-the-results plan.

For example, three students wondered how to support patients at a local children's hospital. They decided there was a need to donate toys, so they created fliers to create awareness and solicit donations, found containers for the donated toys to place in the various classrooms, donated the toys to the hospital—and created a video to share what they accomplished.

Salina's goal is for students to leave as independent self-navigators who have the confidence to make a difference. Projects have included how to create more awareness around the world water shortage; how to prevent school bullying; how to encourage students to play various sports, such as basketball and soccer; how to spread the word about the harmful effects of plastic waste; and what we might learn about the connection between LEGOs and creativity.

Scottish Storyline at the Spence School and Steins Pilar Elementary

Another approach to emergent learning is the Scottish Storyline (Creswell, 1997). (See the Storyline website at https://www.scottish-storyline.com.) According to the Scottish Consultative Council on the Curriculum (n.d.), this process "builds on the key principle that learning, to be meaningful, has to be memorable, and that by using learners' enthusiasm for story-making, the classroom, the teacher's role, and learning can be transformed" (para. 1). The process begins with children creating their own conceptual model, driven by the questions they have about their imagined scene or situation. Stories are written episodically by a class. There is a setting, characters, situations, actions, and outcomes, and the students compare their imagined world to a comparable situation in the real world.

Consider as an example *Elephants Versus Dragons*, developed by Erica Poon-McGovern and her 2nd grade students at the Spence School in New York City. The students, a group of dragons living in the "dragon forest," become concerned by how much of the forest's foliage (the dragons' primary food) is being eaten by the forest's growing population of elephants. Conflicts ensue, and students generate approaches to address them. Poon-McGovern (n.d.) writes that one of her main goals was "to provide my students with opportunities to examine conflict from different perspectives [and] consider the incidents as both the dragons and the elephants" (para. 3).

Scottish Storyline is central to the mission of Oregon's Steins Pilar Elementary School, a magnet school with a focus on experiential learning and quests. The founding principal, Jim Bates, and the instructional coach, Sarah Glann, shared with us how they implement the approach:

> Three times during the academic school year, the storyline approach is developed on each grade level, with each experience lasting two to three months. It is immersive and evolving for each learner. The method has been thoughtfully developed by the international organization, Storyline, and is constant. What changes with each experience are the topic, the focus, and the content. Story is the *common rope*. The teacher presents the students with a challenge, an invitation, or a problem written in a paragraph form. The students understand and are deeply committed to the common rope as the binding agent. As Sarah explained, we say, "When going off in a hundred different directions, you come back to the rope. Stay focused on your inquiries, wherever they take you, but we are all learning together." (Personal correspondence, November 19, 2021)

Two elements are crucial to the Scottish Storyline process. First, students need to get into character: a steward in the wetlands, a paleontologist in the desert, a producer of a Broadway show. Second, the students experience the storyline daily in their simulations of the scenarios and interactions with related experts—a visit from an engineer on the design of future cities or a virtual interview with a zoologist about creating animal habitats. Each student is committed to their character, and this fosters a genuine sense of community. The students at Steins Pilar are living a narrative that connects the curriculum throughout their school day. The teachers are guides in the journey.

Big Picture High Schools

Big Picture Schools are based on the bold vision of co-founders Dennis Littky and Elliot Washor, who created the first school in Rhode Island—Metropolitan Regional Career and Technical Center ("The Met"). The first Met class graduated in 2000, with a 96 percent graduation rate. Ninety-eight percent of its graduates were admitted to postsecondary institutions and received more than $500,000 in scholarships to help fund their college dreams. Currently there are more than 75 Big Picture Schools in the United States and additional sites in Canada, Australia, and the Netherlands.

The Big Picture Learning Network's student-centered learning model is based on the notion that each student is part of an advisory, a learning community of 15 students. With support, each student sets up a personalized program based on their interests, which involves interning with a mentor out in the world. Met students have interned at all kinds of workplaces, from nonprofit organizations to nail salons, from banks and zoos to hospitals and local elementary schools (Littky & Grabelle, 2004). The engagement is pronounced, the situations are 100 percent authentic, and the results are evident as students move on to graduate and achieve postsecondary success.

The 15 Big Picture Schools in Australia now offer the International Big Picture Learning Credential, which creates an interest-based pathway for each student with a wide range of assessments reflecting his or her unique talents and interests (Big Picture Learning Australia, n.d.). Students have focused on such topics as the history of aboriginal peoples, machining, gaming, gender equality, and wellness. Learner achievements are judged on demonstrations and observations of performance using six assessment frames:

- Knowing how to learn
- Empirical reasoning
- Quantitative reasoning
- Social reasoning
- Communication skills
- Personal qualities

The data that result from these assessments are compiled in a learner profile that showcases the student's journey.

ACT

Taking action on emergent narratives lines up with the long-term aims of modern schooling—to develop learners who are connected global citizens, thoughtful and responsive listeners, and courageous and responsible risk takers. These emergent narratives are as true for an algebra classroom tackling such issues as poverty, managing debt, and predicting earthquakes as they are for topics at the elementary school level, such as community helpers, the human body, or courage.

Here are some suggestions for integrating emergent narratives into classroom life.

Make this exploration part of every course.

When educators relegate the exploration of emergent issues to special events (such as capstone experiences, passion projects, and science fairs) or offer them as co-curricular experiences (as part of the debate team, gardening club, or a robotic competition, for instance), they cement inequitable experiences for students.

Co-create satellite spinoff storyboards with students.

Partner with your learners on curricular tributaries originating from the teacher-developed narrative or collaborative storyboards. For example, if students in a world history course are exploring a current event topic on the uprising in Iran sparked by the death of a woman for allegedly not wearing hajib, they might be inspired to do satellite storyboards on the restriction to freedom of expression, the current status of women's rights in various countries, or the Universal Declaration of Human Rights as a means of safeguarding freedom of expression along with others rights. They could share their work in myriad ways: a petition with a call to action, an investigative journalism report, an interactive timeline that captures a series of events, infographics that spotlight freedoms around the world, a virtual symposium featuring international student speakers, and on and on.

Use emergent narrative space wisely.

Given time limits and the need to streamline, teachers need to focus on emergent journeys that are informed by course expectations and whatever seed along that journey that inspired student fascination. Pursuing current topics that are *not* connected to your curriculum can become side trips that have limited value in terms of the goals of your course and the aspirations you have for your students.

Generate fresh ideas.

An emergent narrative, by definition, does not have a tidy end. In fact, this type of narrative may only be in the beginning stages. In our harried lives (a situation that applies to both teachers and students), we often rush too quickly into solutions, judgments, or creations. Harken back to Twyla Tharp's shoebox and Beethoven's journals. There's value in capturing ideas and letting them percolate.

Cultivate a "pitch" mindset.

When students get stuck on the deliverable, they may have missed the point of the emergent narrative in the first place—to explore and make sense of complex, messy, and significant issues. Instead of focusing on the "prettiness" of their learning demonstration, we can celebrate the fact that they have deepened their knowledge, expanded their networks, and reflected over the course of the journey. You can model this "pitch" mindset, develop it with your students, and coach it based on their sketches.

Offer authentic assessments.

The pitch-to-pitch model goes beyond the school walls to enlist people with expertise in a given topic or challenge. This reinforces the connection to authenticity; students see *why* what they're doing is important, get clarity on *who* they're trying to influence, and learn how form (e.g., infographics, blueprint, podcast) can be employed to best advocate, inform, and share with different audiences. Feedback from those in the know helps students with the *how* of the deliverable.

In Our Next Episode . . .

All curriculum needs fresh air. When students are reflecting on what matters most to them in the larger world, the ground is fertile for seeding quests and pitching ideas for a purposeful and rewarding narrative. In the next episode, we will look at how learners can apply the pitch-to-pitch model when designing and pursuing their own inquiries and how to translate a student-driven query directly into a storyboard.

Episode 11

Student-Initiated Storyboards

Learning Target	Engage	Examine	Act
We can help students create and fulfill their own learning narratives.	Explore how students can launch a meaningful pitch leading to a storyboard narrative.	Examine the four-phase pitch-to-pitch model to design a student narrative.	Craft a storyboard template to capture the student-led narrative, seeking opportunities for implementation.

ENGAGE

A group of elementary students at the Denver Montessori School in Colorado learned about the many children in Zambia who were dying from malaria as a result of mosquito bites—and they were motivated to take action. The Zambian children lacked netting that would protect them while they slept. The elementary students worked with school staff, as well as with local and global partners, to develop a solution inspired by the netting used for toy bins and collapsible laundry baskets. This multiyear project resulted in a coordinated effort to make and ship their product to Zambian partners.

When a student pitches an investigation emerging from a point of fascination, a learning journey begins. For example, public high school student Nikhil Goyal was fed up with the one-size-fits-all school culture in the United States. He decided to write a book that featured interviews with a range of international education experts, including Grant Wiggins, Alfie Kohn, and Will Richardson. That book, *Schools on Trial* (2016), ended up being published by Doubleday. This 17-year-old aspiring author reached out to these experts and presented himself and his aims in such a way that they took the time to assist.

Whether it's protecting kids from malaria or seeking to improve schools, challenges such as these can be painfully real, globally connected, or personally aspirational; they can be ripped from the headlines or inspired by timeless patterns.

So how can a learner lay out a storyboard when the narrative is unfolding?

Priming the Pump for a Pitch

Inviting students to the design table makes their thinking visible, encourages creative thinking, and develops essential storytelling skills. However, many learners are not accustomed to identifying and pursuing an emergent area of fascination, curiosity, or challenge. They may struggle with what to do when the path is unpredictable as a result of volatility, uncertainty, complexity, and ambiguity.

There's value here in exploring what entrepreneurs do. In the face of an unknown future, they simply act. They don't try to analyze uncertainty, or plan for every contingency, or predict the outcomes (Schlesinger et al., 2012). Allison had the opportunity to collaborate with Eric Chagala, principal of the Vista Innovation and Design

Academy (VIDA), and Charlie Keifer, a Fortune 500 consultant, to apply entrepreneurial thinking to learner-generated actions. With this kind of work in mind, consider the following questions:

- **Do I really want to look into this? Do I care enough to take action?** People need some level of motivation to compel them to act.
- **What smart step can I take?** Learners can do many things with what they already have at their disposal. They can find out more information, design an initial sketch, or listen to other perspectives to build understanding.
- **What am I learning? Is this a promising direction?** Every action produces change. Reflecting on possible results will affect next steps and boost motivation.
- **How can I build on what I know now?** In this part of the iterative cycle, learners commit to continuing the challenge, seeking out others in the know, and sharing expertise.

Figure 11.1 elaborates on the process of growing an entrepreneurial idea. The cycle consists of four elements—desire, act, learn, and build—and is designed to guide students as they begin this work. The explanation column provides context and motivates students; the reflective questions, which we mirrored above, get them moving in the right direction; and the learning column consists of results framed as "I can" statements, such as "I can listen to and empathize with others to imagine what I could do to help." Although the figure is laid out linearly here, it's designed to be an iterative cycle.

How can we help learners develop an idea that will have a positive effect on others—personally, locally, or globally? In the section that follows, we offer two graphic organizers that support students as they develop and document their own emergent narratives.

EXAMINE

In the previous episode, we called your attention to four phases in our pitch-to-pitch model (see Figure 10.1, p. 136):

- Launching and formulating the pitch
- Investigating sketches for action
- Creating the deliverable
- Revising a pitch or developing a new one

FIGURE 11.1

Growing an Entrepreneurial Idea

Cycle	Explanation	Reflective Questions	Learning
Desire	You uncover something you want to learn, improve, or have an effect on. All you need is sufficient desire to get started and the optimism that you can make a difference.	• Do I really want to look into this topic? • Do I have sufficient desire to get started (and to stick with it)?	I can listen to and empathize with others to imagine what actions might help. I can get excited about the possibilities of an idea as I sketch out and share my thinking.
Act	You start by taking action. You do this by making little bets to get something out into the world by asking questions, listening intently, making observations, and generating ideas.	• What's a smart step I could take right now at nearly no cost?	I can identify and execute a small step that is informed by what I am learning.
Learn	Every time you act, reality changes. You more clearly understand the quality of an idea by putting ideas out into the world. We do this through observations, testing, or audience reaction. Sometimes the step you take gets you nearer to what you want, and sometimes what you want changes.	• Are you optimistic that this is a promising direction? • Did those actions get you closer to your desire? • What do you need to draw even closer? • Do you still want this enough to continue?	I can examine data or results to look for patterns based on the actions I took. I can step back and reflect to see the situation through another's perspective.
Build	You change course as needed to act on what you have learned. And you bring others along to continue to build on what you created.	• How has my understanding changed? What did I learn about what I want? • How did I empathize with others to care about the idea? • How do I bring other people along to invest in the idea? What are the next steps I/we might take?	I can think flexibly with others about immediate possibilities and next steps. I can grow ideas with others to help shape my plan, expand my thinking, and expand my network.

Source: Copyright 2020 by Allison Zmuda. Used with permission.

When students are laying out an aspiration, challenge, or idea, the goal is to show the internal connections within each set of experiences.

Students should identify the actions they have taken in each phase of the process, noting their observations along the way. They can reflect—in writing or via images or audio recordings—on the sources they used, their data-gathering processes, and the actions they considered that ultimately fueled the narrative. The journey should tell the story of the learning that took place, the surprises along the way, and the experience from end to end.

As you are reading this section, consider how you might begin to open this up with students. The idea is not only to inspire them to wonder but also to provide a few parameters to launch this self-directed inquiry and actions. Figure 11.2 shows a pitch-to-pitch model we created, based on a project implemented by a student who was inspired to improve his high school's baseball field (Finerman, 2022). The student chose to tackle a problem—the need for dugouts and new fencing. The scale was local, with emphasis on the community, and the audience for the pitch consisted of the players on the team and the spectators who would be attending the games. In the investigation phase, the student worked with a construction company, a landscape architect, and local funding groups. The deliverable was a remodeled and improved playing field. Note that the storyboard this student created includes before-and-after images of the field, as well as a news article that was published subsequent to project completion.

Figure 11.3 shows a second example, inspired by a curriculum project Heidi worked on with 5th graders. The students also tackled a problem they had read about in the local newspaper: how to help newly arrived immigrant students more easily adjust to school. The 5th graders decided to work with a local branch of the Integrated Refugee and Immigration Services (IRIS), which was located just a block from their elementary school. The deliverable involved working with an immigrant family and interacting regularly with their children. One student involved not only made new friends but also found an idea to pitch—exploring careers in service.

ACT

When students are learning with storyboards they initiate themselves, it's not always clear how the process will unfold or where new inquiries will lead. While this open-endedness may disarm some students, clarifying the phases of a learning journey can provide helpful signposts.

FIGURE 11.2

A Student-Initiated Storyboard: Example A

Pitch to Pitch: Student Improves Local Baseball Fields

THE PITCH

Genre (Problem)

I want to improve the high school baseball field with dugouts and new fencing. I want to do this in time for the new season.

Source

While practicing, I noticed that the existing field was in need of repair and upkeep.

Scale

This is a LOCAL project, with emphasis on my community.

THE INVESTIGATION

Research Actions

- Assess NEED to improve the dugouts and field on the basis of interviews with coaches and players.
- Work with a local construction company and landscape architect to determine the PROCESS and STEPS for improvement.
- Work with FUNDRAISING groups to develop a plan.

Networks

- Construction company
- School board
- Special extended-learning opportunity class

THE DELIVERABLE

Form

Proposed plan and remodeled and improved playing field and dugouts

Fundraising

Resulted in $15,000 in donations

Audience

Players on the baseball team and spectators

Impact

Improved performance for players, as well as satisfaction and comfort

THE REFLECTION

Comments

This started off just as a quick idea like, "Oh, what if we did this?" After working, it just ended up being better than even I expected.

Thinking About the Future

I am interested in working in construction and real estate after graduating

FIGURE 11.3

A Student-Initiated Storyboard: Example B

Pitch to Pitch: 5th Grader Helps New Arrivals Adjust to School

THE PITCH

Genre (Problem)

(Problem) How to help newly arrived immigrant children make an easier adjustment to the school and community.

Source

Concern about the children of new immigrants in our community; an article on this issue in the local newspaper.

Scale

LOCAL and GLOBAL

THE INVESTIGATION

Research Actions

- Identify a specific family, learn about their experiences, and find ways to help their children.
- Read about the experience of newly arrived immigrants.
- Interview Integrated Refugee and Immigrant Services (IRIS) staff about ways to help.

Networks

- Our local IRIS headquarters located near school
- UNICEF
- Local Chamber of Commerce

Resources

Booklist at socialjusticebooks.org

THE DELIVERABLE

Form

Service: I will work through the school year with an immigrant family with children. Each week, I will connect with the children, just to talk and see how they're doing.

Product

I will create a photo timeline of our experience, with pictures and captions.

Audience

The children of the family

Impact

I hope the children will report that their transition goes well, that they're happy, and that I have helped.

THE REFLECTION

Comments

This was an incredible year for me learning about the family and, especially, becoming friends with their children. Each week I learned more about their challenges. It made me appreciate so many things in my life. I wish the project could go on.

I will stay in touch with the children. I have made friends.

I also learned what the IRIS people do to help. That's something I'd like to think about doing when I grow up. I might want to pitch an idea about careers in service for my next project.

Phase 1: Launching and Formulating the Pitch

What motivates a student to pursue a problem, investigate an issue, propose a solution, generate an artistic expression, dive into research, or even ask questions is individual and situational. **Sources** for a pitch might emerge from experiences with family and friends or from considering the aspirational goals and mission of the school. Along with Bena Kallick, we crafted the following long-term aims that encourage the quest for a meaningful pitch.

Learners should

- Investigate challenging contemporary global and local issues by pursuing a given question or line of thinking.
- Use design thinking and other processes to develop solutions, findings, prototypes, performances, and media.
- Navigate diverse sources and perspectives to make discerning and thoughtful judgments.
- Generate, enrich, and craft communication through the strategic use of evidence and a command of language.
- Share stories, ideas, and points of view to engage others to think interdependently and act collectively.
- Think flexibly, take responsible risks, and listen with understanding and empathy as they engage with the world (Habits of Mind Institute, 2016).

News and media sources can suggest a pitch. Noteworthy is Newsela, which offers a free database of quality nonfiction articles from a variety of trusted sources, such as the *New York Times* and *Scientific American*. These not only expand a student's grasp of the world but also are available at adjustable Lexile levels. A pitch might also be an offshoot from the ongoing curriculum when a particular topic has prompted fascination. Imagine, for example, a 4th grader studying bird migration patterns in science class who becomes captivated by the video technology utilized in the movie *Winged Migration* and goes on to explore who makes these specialized cameras and how they are mounted on birds to capture such vivid footage of birds in flight.

In addition to the source, learners should consider two other elements when formulating their pitch: **genre** and **scale**. Will they frame the pitch as a topic, an issue, a problem, a theme, or a case study? The lens the student selects will open a range of possibilities. Of course, the genre might change or fuse with another genre as the investigation unfolds. For example, a pitch that starts as an exploration of the topic of climate change might develop into a case study that incorporates historical documentation of how the climate in the student's home community has changed over the past 100 years.

The audience for the pitch will likely be the teacher, a group of teachers, or a group of students. It also could extend to field experts, business or community leaders who value fresh thinking on complex problems and are energized by the resourcefulness, generative thinking, and commitment of students. Learners need to consider these questions before presenting their pitch:

- Am I clearly communicating my idea?
- Have I established the need to pursue this idea? Why is it worthy of more exploration? What parts are compelling?
- Am I presenting the information, stories, and illustrations in a way that promotes growing networks of collaboration?
- What methods am I using to make the pitch compelling?
- How does my audience shape the content and tone of my pitch?
- What supporting visuals or media will help clarify my message?

If the pitch is approved and ready to launch, the student can move to sketching actions for investigation. If the pitch is rejected and needs total revision, it's a great opportunity for growth.

Phase 2: Investigating Sketches for Action

Once the pitch has received the go-ahead, students can lay out the possibilities for actions that they have sketched to determine which are the most viable and compelling. They're leading the research. They will need to identify resources that will assist them; these may include various organizations, information centers, and websites, as well as print and online media.

Students should try to create or join networks with other researchers who are interested in their field of pursuit. To enlist support, they should join forces with other students in a class, or they might seek out and establish connections, growing networks around an idea with local or virtual communities. For example, that student studying local climate change might contact the local library or science organizations and interview senior citizens to capture their recollections of what the climate used to be like.

Phase 3: Creating the Deliverable

A deliverable could be a product, a performance, a service, or an experience. A **product** is tangible. Whether it takes the form of written text, an image, a report, a graphic, a model, or a prototype, it should match the intention of the quest and the needs of the intended audience. For example, the audience might be readers of written work, users on a website, a board reviewing a proposed plan, an expert reviewing a prototype, gallery visitors, or users of a new gadget or appliance. The possibilities are unlimited.

A **performance** is temporal; it's the act of staging or presenting for spectators some form of entertainment. We can certainly record a dance, music, an athletic performance, a speech, a debate, a play, or another demonstration, but watching a video is not the same as experiencing a live performance. The audience for a performance might be an individual or a group, and it might be staged in an auditorium, a stadium, a rehearsal room, or a park.

A **service** should be based on an audience's specific needs in a specific context. If there's a train station in town, for example, a learner might create a children's guide to train travel that might be made available to young travelers boarding at the station. A service might also be generated in response to a request from an individual or organization. For example, a senior citizen center might generate a request for high school students to collaborate with patrons on a storytelling hour. The audience is central here; the student must prepare a service that matches the need.

In the course of determining a pitch, a clear deliverable and audience may not always materialize. In that case, the **experience** itself can be a worthy outcome. The process should be viewed as an opportunity—preparation for real situations. The audience in this instance is the learner.

Phase 4: Revising a Pitch or Developing a New One

Reflecting on feedback from the deliverable is crucial; here, learners review the totality of the experience. They reflect on whether their exploration altered their expectations from the initial pitch or, conversely, reinforced them. They consider how the genre and scale of the project influenced the deliverable. Most important, they consider how they might revise the deliverable to improve its quality and impact or whether they must develop a new pitch entirely. For example, a group of students might have decided to create a small business that connects neighborhood residents experiencing food insecurity with low-cost meals prepared in the high school's culinary arts program. Once the students have reflected on their pitch, they might modify the program offerings to focus on different kinds of food items or adjust the initial marketing plan to include a deal where the first delivery is free.

In Our Next Episode . . .

This episode focused on students designing and developing their own emergent narratives through a student-initiated storyboard. Our final episode will look at how to engage families in understanding and participating in the student's journey.

Episode 12

Sharing Curriculum Narratives with Families

Learning Target	Engage	Examine	Act
We can communicate curriculum narratives to families to promote connection.	Explore the need for transparency and connection in sharing curriculum with families.	Review examples to identify the applicability and value to your classroom and school practices of sharing curriculum with families.	Create or revise family curriculum communications.

ENGAGE

What kind of access to curriculum do schools provide families right now? We asked this question on LinkedIn, and the overwhelming response was that families had access to "all of it." However, when examining school districts around the world, we found that publicly available information was typically limited to the following:

- A philosophy statement for the grade level or subject area
- A program of studies with a brief description of each course
- A collection of external curriculum standards
- A cursory outline of topics the course would cover

In our current political climate, many school leaders worry that revealing too much of the curriculum to the public will generate a firestorm. But many family members feel left in the dark as to what their children are investigating and creating. They rely on asking their children for information, reviewing their child's assignments, and approaching individual classroom teachers for clarification.

Families deserve to know more about the curriculum so they can meaningfully address their children's school experiences at home. Providing a preview into what students are learning is a show of respect to our families. Doing so in a way that is accessible—through invitational language, brief overviews, illustrations, and multiple representations—signifies that the school values families as partners in learning.

So how might you describe curricular ideas to a diverse group of families with a range of backgrounds, preconceived notions, areas of interest, and beliefs about schooling? How might you get families excited about the curriculum journey? What is most important to share to provide a window into the learning experience?

First, consider the following guidelines for crafting messages to families about curriculum:

- **Be respectful.** Using the word *family* is more inclusive than simply referring to *parents*. Clarify your purpose for communicating.
- **Be invitational.** Use engaging and accessible language in your communications. Provide links so families can give feedback, ask questions, or request information.
- **Keep it simple.** Streamline communication to focus on the essentials.

EXAMINE

Figure 12.1 illustrates the typical approach schools use to inform families about curriculum programs. Although philosophy statements, programs of studies, lists of standards, and course outlines do provide some information (see the "How It Helps" column in Figure 12.1), families often ask themselves, *What is this course* really *about? What will students actually be doing?* The information signaled in the "What Is Missing" column provides some answers. Schools could more clearly show how a course aligns to broader goals, what compelling questions students are tackling, and how students are applying their learning.

Try this yourself. Go on a reconnaissance mission to find out what information about the curriculum is currently available to families in your school or in your child's school. What did you uncover?

If schools want families to be more supportive of what their children are learning, they need to create refreshed lines of communication. The following three ideas can provide more clarity and deepen school-family partnerships.

FIGURE 12.1

Approaches to Informing Families About Curriculum

Current Approach	How It Helps	What Is Missing
Philosophy statement	Clarifies the pedagogy and instructional approach that families can anticipate the school using for their children	Often silent on how curriculum units serve the philosophy or align with broader goals (e.g., external standards, Portrait of a Graduate, Habits of Mind)
Program of studies	Provides a concise overview of the course	Often silent on compelling questions, topics, or creations students will engage in
List of standards addressed within each unit or course	Demonstrates alignment to external curriculum frameworks	Often silent on specific topics, compelling questions, and authentic applications of learning
Outline of topics to cover	Identifies general topics that are the basis of a course or curriculum unit	Often silent on curriculum narrative—how units connect with one another and what students are capable of doing (applying what they know)

Making Curriculum Storyboards Public

We're proposing, of course, the use of curriculum storyboards, a fresh idea that we're drafting here. Some schools, faced with this issue of communicating with parents about curriculum, have had similar concerns and have come up with solutions to address those concerns. For example, Allison had the privilege to be part of a multiyear curriculum renewal project in Connecticut's Madison Public Schools. District leaders wanted to explain their approach to families and provide updated K–12 course revisions. In an interview with Assistant Superintendent Gail Dahling-Hench, she explained why it's important to give families a window into classrooms with publicly posted curricula:

> We believe that the best curriculum is not a package that is purchased, but a curriculum that is developed by teachers and is responsive to the community it serves. It's our professional responsibility to educate each student in both the content and skills defined in our Madison Profile of a Graduate. We will best accomplish that mission with the support and engagement of our families. Our units are constructed with specific Madison Public Schools criteria to mindfully build on prior content standards and demonstrate transfer in performance-based assessments. The curriculum, which is posted on our website, offers every parent and student the opportunity to see the aspirations of each discipline. It also tells the story of how the learning relates to prior units, as well as the new transfer, knowledge, and skills that will be acquired in the current unit. Families, tutors, and students can use the information on our website to prepare for learning, deepen their unit experience, and be partners in success. This visibility is our promise to provide an equally compelling educational experience for every child. (Personal communication, July 13, 2022)

The curriculum of Madison Public Schools is posted online (www.madison.k12.ct.us/district/curriculum-instruction). If a parent wants to see what their child will be exploring in any subject, they can navigate to the appropriate grade level and see the units of instruction for the year. The district uses a common template for curriculum, with each unit organized around the same key components: desired results/key understandings; standards or goals; transfer (what students will be able to use their learning for); meaning (what students will understand and what essential questions they will consider); and acquisition of knowledge and skill (what students will know and be skilled at doing). The curriculum designers have also included brief video snippets to share some highlights of what students will be exploring and creating.

In spring 2020, when the pandemic caused many schools to move to remote learning, Madison Public Schools found that it could quickly modify its assessment and learning plans—and get that information out to students and families—because of the website's ease of use and the valuable information it provided. In addition to the work in Google Classroom, the K–12 website posted weekly distance learning modules that further informed parents and students of the objectives, plans, and intended outcomes for that week. Madison reported that pre-pandemic, approximately 2,000 users visited the site each month; throughout the pandemic, that number increased by 1,000. Families in the district are now accustomed to visiting the district site to get curriculum updates. It has become a trusted resource for families and educators alike.

As we began to prototype curriculum storyboards in 2021, we realized that engaging small focus groups starts to build an understanding of *what* a curriculum narrative is, *why* it is powerful, and *how* it can impact connections. When Virginia Beach City Public Schools in Virginia ran a series of focus groups with families and students to get feedback on their curriculum storyboards under development, students commented that there were "good images" and that the storyboards were "easier to read and understand," "straight to the point," and "well organized." They wondered about "using bold typeface to highlight important words," "how teachers were going to adapt to this," "who to go to for questions about the curriculum story," and "whether the pictures really captivate the curriculum."

Parents echoed many of what students said about the storyboards' clear organization and high-quality images. They also "loved the idea of having a glimpse of what the year will look like" and appreciated "having essential questions to get kids and parents talking" and "unit titles that are catchy and sound fun." Overall, parents' responses expressed excitement and highlighted practical concerns:

- Could the storyboard format be consistent across subjects and grades?
- Could the district do more to explain how the topics build on one another throughout the year?
- Would the storyboard approach apply to every child's learning at school?

- How would the district make these storyboards available? Would print copies be available? Could they be accessed via links on the individual school websites?
- Would parents receive training or guidance on how to best use storyboards with their children?
- What could families do at home to encourage and support their students' learning? Would there be a place on the storyboard for family connections and resources? The district went on to use a number of the parents' questions to shape large-scale field-testing and implementation of the storyboard approach.

Dr. Kipp Rogers, chief academic officer of Virginia Beach City Public Schools, shared the positive reception curriculum storyboards received from students, teachers, principals, families, senior staff, and school board members. "The storyboards," he said, "demystify what is being taught in the classroom and help everyone better understand the connection between units throughout the school year." Members of the district's senior staff team indicated that the storyboards clarify how the curriculum showcases the manner in which the district is working to help students own and be able to transfer their learning—all part of efforts to make students future-ready. One key piece of feedback obtained from the process was that the storyboards make the curriculum more transparent and invited more substantive conversation among school leaders, families, and students. Parents who might have been feeling uncertain about what was being taught in their child's classroom could more easily see and understand the broader context of the course, which supported better communication with their child and their child's teacher.

Reimagining the Syllabus

College professor Aaron S. Richmond (2016) noted the need to make his course syllabus more learner centered—so he reimagined it. Richmond, a professor of educational psychology and human development, focuses on using "warm and friendly" language in his syllabus to build rapport and connect with his students. For example, in the section on learning resources for students, he writes, "Each class is different. Sometimes we need a little help from one another to learn how to study for a test or complete an assignment. If you need help, please do not hesitate to come and talk to me" (p. 2).

We were inspired to develop a version more applicable to a preK–12 classroom. We designed Figure 12.2 as a self-assessment tool to help users assess whether key syllabus content and language are family friendly. The tool focuses on three areas: classroom culture and family connections, student roles and responsibilities, and evaluation and assessment. As you can see, all comments are expressed as "I" statements, such as, "I communicate with families to share student highlights, connect to learning opportunities, and build relationships." It's also helpful to reflect with families toward the end of the course; schools can use their feedback to improve curricular communications going forward.

Now that you have looked over the tool, what connections are you making to your own practice? What criteria might you want to include to strengthen communication with students and families?

Sending Letters to Families

In 2015, Avon Public Schools in Connecticut began sending out family letters at the start of each course unit. The original concern was to address significant changes to the curriculum in English language arts and mathematics because of alignment to the Common Core State Standards, the adoption of new resources, and the shift toward collaborative curriculum development.

Curriculum writers developed family letters for each unit that provided clarity about the expectations and approach. Figure 12.3 shows a letter sent home to the families of 8th graders describing a math unit focused on comparing, analyzing, and composing 2-D and 3-D shapes. The teacher explains the instructional focus, as well as what families can do to support their child's learning, such as constructing various 3-D shapes at home. The letters increased fidelity among teachers in their instructional approach, as well as in how they reviewed student work in their common planning meetings.

ACT

Here are some actions you can take to improve communications with families about your curriculum.

Solicit family feedback.

Sometimes in our rush to design a better solution, we skip over the needs and frustrations of the end user. The first step of design thinking is to listen with

FIGURE 12.2

Self-Assessment Tool: How Connection-Centered Is My Classroom Practice?

Evaluative Criteria	NOT YET	YES
Classroom Culture and Family Connections		
I write all curriculum and lessons to be clear, accessible, and family friendly. *(e.g., curriculum storyboards, learning sets, unit letters to families)*		
I explain how I ensure a safe and nurturing environment, with clear expectations for how we work together and treat one another. *(e.g., "We generate new ideas and build on the thinking of one another. This classroom is a safe place where we listen and work to better understand others' ideas and perspectives.")*		
I share multiple methods for students and families seeking further support. *(e.g., email contact information, text message information, posting regular office hours for scheduled or drop-in visits).*		
I communicate with families to share student highlights, connect to learning opportunities, and build relationships.		
Roles and Responsibilities		
I encourage my students to participate in developing and monitoring yearlong policies and procedures for class.		
I encourage my students to share connections and resources related to the unit or course explorations.		
I clarify what I expect of both my students and myself as their teacher.		
I partner with my students to develop student voice, co-creation, social construction, and self-discovery.		
I regularly examine local and global events to update or revise the selection of topics, the design of storylines, and the opportunity for investigation and creation.		
Evaluation and Assessment		
I use learning targets aligned to standards to show evidence of student growth.		
I guide learners to self-assess and monitor their progress in relation to learning targets.		
I provide regular and actionable feedback to and with learners.		
I share and develop quality criteria with my students in advance of their work to ensure their understanding.		
I design authentic assessments to provide opportunities for student exploration, creation for a target audience, and progress monitoring.		

FIGURE 12.3

Letter About a Math Unit Sent to the Families of 8th Graders

Dear Families,

Our Focus:

We are starting our eighth math unit, which focuses on comparing, analyzing, and composing 2-D and 3-D shapes. The students will expand their prior knowledge of shape identification from unit two (triangles, rectangles, squares, circles, hexagons, cubes, cylinders, spheres, and cones) to explore shapes on a deeper level.

Instructional Focus:

Students will identify shapes as two dimensional (lying in a plane, "flat") or three dimensional ("solid"). They will be able to analyze and compare two- and three-dimensional shapes in different sizes and orientations, using informal language to describe their similarities; their differences; their parts (e.g., the number of sides and vertices/"corners"); and other attributes (e.g., having sides of equal length). Students will model shapes that appear in the world by building them. They will also draw and compose simple shapes to form larger shapes.

Here's how you can support your child's learning at home:

- Play with pattern blocks or tangrams.
- Construct 3-D shapes with objects such as playdough, marshmallows, pretzels, straws, etc.
- Search for and identify shapes in the environment.

3-D Shapes

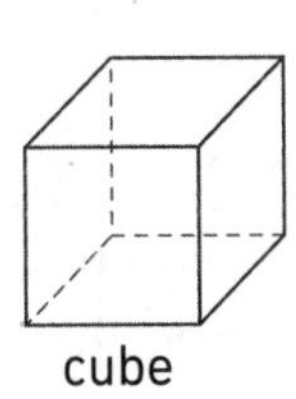

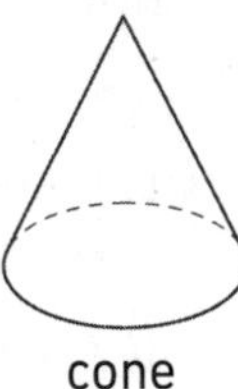

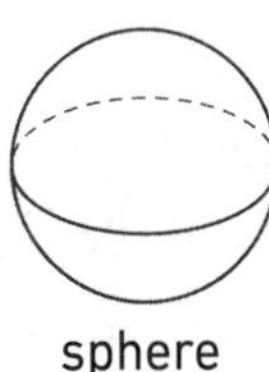

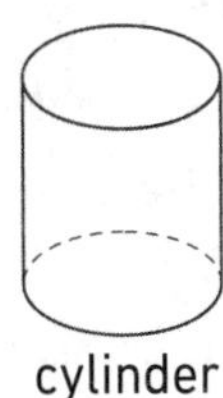

Source: Avon Public Schools, Avon, Connecticut. Used with permission.

understanding and empathy to clarify problems. Often schools send out emails or flyers requesting information. Sometimes they will put a notice in a child's backpack. What is important here is to consider ways to expand the possibility for obtaining useful and honest feedback. For example, the family letters may work for some, but others might prefer a short video sharing the same content. Still others might find it helpful to receive several newsletter updates along the way on how the unit is progressing; these updates might answer such questions as, *What are students immersed in or excited about? What compelling questions are students exploring in their research? What creations are they working on as they become more skillful and sophisticated?* Updates could be just a few sentences long, or they could take the form of quick video snippets or photographs with captions. This newsletter practice becomes especially significant if students produce it themselves as a regular reflection that captures the deepening connections within their learning and their growing skill sets.

Establish criteria for communicating about the curriculum.

The goal is to give families a consistent, a coherent, and an accessible explanation of the curriculum. Set up a few key criteria. Here are some examples:

- **Be consistent.** Teachers provide a general overview of their course, which they will supplement throughout the year in a consistent format. This consistency makes it easier for families to navigate.
- **Focus on coherence.** Teachers provide a year-at-a-glance overview of each unit, showing how the various units connect to one another (horizontal alignment). Ideally, families would also have an understanding of vertical alignment. For example, families should be able to see the key priorities of their child's middle school science classes—and how those same priorities play out in grades 6, 7, and 8. In Indiana's Childs Elementary School (n.d.), eight core concepts drive integrated study throughout the elementary International Baccalaureate Primary Years Program curriculum: form, function, causation, change, connection, perspective, responsibility, and reflection.
- **Ensure accessibility.** Teachers describe their curriculum in clear and family-friendly language. They use visual cues to illustrate core content and clarify how students will make meaning of that content.

Reexamine communications from the start.

During the early days of school, consider refreshing some of the ways you share curriculum with families. Review how you present your courses, your expectations, and your instructional approach. Do these help families become more oriented to the course content? Do they lay the groundwork for improved interactions? For example, you might use a syllabus not only to frame curriculum content but also to give parents a view into classroom connections, assessment practices, and teacher and student roles. You might hold a series of focus groups where parents can clarify what information is most helpful to them and in which formats.

Provide multiple views of the curriculum storyboard on your school website.

Family members may want to see which compelling questions their child is exploring or the kinds of assessments teachers will ask students to do. It's relatively easy for you or your school's information technology department to design a drop-down view for families to see more detail if they so choose. For example, your school could offer a four-level view of the curriculum:

- Level 1: Course title and overarching questions; unit title, focus of the story, and image cues
- Level 2: Key standards framed as learning targets
- Level 3: Summative and authentic assessments
- Level 4: Core resources for school and home

Another approach might offer a brief overview of the unit that focuses on what students will explore, investigate, or create. Users could click on various links to find a more detailed overview of unit goals that shows their alignment to external frameworks. This could be a blend of family-friendly and educator-friendly language.

Listen with empathy to parent/family concerns.

When sharing the narratives organized in curriculum storyboards and learning sets, keep in mind that this may be the first time that parents have seen the curriculum described in family-friendly language. Now that they better understand the curricular approach, they may want to raise questions, share their perspective, or suggest additional resources.

For a start, they may be unfamiliar with the concept of *curriculum as narrative.* Consider revisiting key ideas in Episode 4 about the brain-friendly nature of a story and how it helps students engage, examine, and take action. Parents also may benefit from a quick video tutorial that shows them how to read the curriculum storyboard and learning sets.

Families may take issue with the approach or focus of the narrative if, for example, they don't understand the flow of units across the year in math or even the importance of the focus of a particular unit of study on place value. Engage them in productive conversation to better understand their family perspective, expertise, and aspirations for their children. This is also a reason to include them in developing and refining modern learner goals. If they understand and value the learner goals, there's greater potential they will buy into a narrative that aligns with those goals.

Finally, they may just have a different view of what teaching and learning should be or how their children learn best. They may wonder how your approach aligns with what they believe postsecondary institutions want, or they may be concerned because it differs from how they experienced schooling. When parents insist on a change (or insist that things *don't* change), listening intently with curiosity will go a long way. Rather than justifying your approach or passing judgment on a parent's view, ask thoughtful questions to open up lines of reflection and connection. Use prompts like "Tell me more," or "I think you're saying. . . ," or "So, I'm hearing that you would like. . . ." Ask, "Is there anything else I need to know?" to get more detail. These questions and commentary provide an opportunity to reflect and clarify.

Families want to know what their children are studying in school. Storyboards—with their common format, accessible language, concise overviews, and compelling ideas—not only give families this key information but also help them enjoy their child's learning journey throughout the school year. They can ask better questions about the curriculum and be better learning partners for their child and their child's teachers.

Epilogue: The Story Continues

Now it's time for your own hero's journey.

Perhaps you and your colleagues are ready to shift away from coverage and develop curriculum storyboards and learning sets guided by the ideas in this book. Perhaps you're a school or district administrator who has been motivated by the broader vision framed by modern learner roles and are now equipped to rally your school community to reimagine your goals and your Portrait of a Graduate. Perhaps you're an instructional leader, a department chair, or a professional learning community leader who will make the shift with your professional colleagues to develop coherent, vertically aligned, and dynamic curriculum documents framed as narrative. Perhaps you're an individual teacher who wants to pitch new learning opportunities for your students as they examine the phenomena in their world.

Regardless of your position, this change will require reflective deliberation, thoughtful action, and courage on your part. We want to wrap up by addressing two questions: *How urgent is the need to streamline?* and *How can we bring a range of perspectives to the process?*

Because we're generating new knowledge in every field every day, the need for streamlining is not going away. We're also witnessing tremendous growth in the field of education in terms of fresh pedagogy, approaches, tools, platforms, and strategies. This constant change and growth are key reasons for our emphasis on emergent learning and phenomena-based curriculum. Access, networking, and media making will continue to be front and center for our students. They will need to develop the skills required to respond enthusiastically and intelligently to this ever-changing world. Schools will undoubtedly look different in 20 years.

For schools to move forward, they need a fresh and shared approach to deciding what matters most and how to engage students. Each school has its own setting, faces its own challenges, and needs to take into account various points of view. At the heart of curriculum planning are focused conversations with colleagues across grade levels and vertically; this is necessary because emerging narratives in each course have implications for other teachers who share (or will someday share) the same students. Further, we must listen carefully to students and families and encourage their insights. This is a collaborative and inclusive journey.

Harken back to the classic hero's journey of Odysseus, who encountered many obstacles in *The Odyssey,* including the Cyclops, the Sirens, and a violent storm conjured by Poseidon. Whenever there is heroic conflict, there will be challenge, a battle, and a victor. Odysseus survives his journey with the aid of others, notably Athena and Telemachus, and, in the journeying, expands and deepens his view of what matters most in life. As we noted in this book's Prologue, narratives end with a resolution: the hero reflecting on lessons learned from the challenges that were faced. This resolution does not necessarily mean that all the challenges were successfully addressed; there were likely stumbles and failures along the way. But even if the journey doesn't take us exactly where we thought we wanted to go, it is still a success if it leads to growth, generates optimism for the future, and builds an appetite for new adventures.

That's what we aim for in shifting from a static view of curriculum coverage to the dynamic injection of storylines. We take on the roles of creative writers, composers, and storytellers and deal in what matters most, what is relevant, and what inspires the young people in our classrooms. With the help of colleagues, families, and students, we can choose to shift our perspectives on how we shape curriculum narratives, how we develop authentic assessments, and how we write learning sets so the students in our care can engage with the future with courage and creativity.

> But you, brave and adept from this day on . . . there's hope that you will reach your goal. The journey that stirs you now is not far off.
>
> —Homer, *The Odyssey*

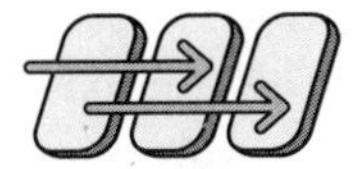

Acknowledgments

Syncopation. Over the past three years, the two of us found a rhythm writing together. Up with the roosters in the morning, we discussed curriculum and composition, icons and accessibility, streamlining and creativity. The backdrop to this work was the whirlwind force of the pandemic affecting the lives of kids, families, teachers, and schools. Shaping this book has been a journey of its own. We are keenly aware of key people who directly contributed to our syncopation and made it possible, and we extend our thanks to them:

- **American International Schools in the Americas** (AMISA), with special thanks to Dereck Rhoads and Adam Slaton for their early and enthusiastic support of our work.
- **Colegio Maya de Guatemala** (Guatemala), with gratitude for Jeff Fifield and the staff, who were happy to begin prototyping the curriculum design as part of their overall curriculum articulation.
- **Denton Independent School District** (Texas), with special thanks to Emily Thompson for her curriculum storyboard and leaders Lisa Thibodeaux and Sandra Brown for seeing the possibilities of this work.
- **Humble Independent School District** (Texas), with special thanks to Ann Johnson and ISD professional development team.
- **Lincoln School: The American International School of Buenos Aires** (Argentina), for their tremendous contribution and collaboration with the ALLs. Special thanks to Madeleine Heide and the school's leadership team.

- **Little Elm Independent School District** (Texas), with special thanks to Michelle Wood for her curriculum storyboard, Penny Trammel for her leadership, and the early prototyping the district's curriculum leaders have started.
- **New Haven Public Magnet Schools** (Connecticut), for their inspiration on the seeds for learning sets, specifically Michelle Bonnano and Sabrina Breland.
- **Pennsylvania ASCD and Virginia ASCD,** especially Deanna Mayers and Laurie McCullough, for being early supporters of the work.
- **St. Louis Archdiocese Schools (Missouri)** leadership, with special gratitude to Maureen Lovette and Anthony VanGessel.
- **St. Stephen's and St. Agnes School** (Virginia), particularly the leadership of Lana Shea, the powerful storyboard contribution of Michelle Bruch, and the faculty who are starting to protoype examples.
- **Virginia Beach City Public Schools** (Virginia), whose embrace of curriculum storyboards to provide a window into learning continues to inspire. Thank you to Nancye Flynne and G. Thomas Coker Jr. for their curriculum storyboards; Chief Academic Officer Kipp Rogers; Division Directors Lorena Kelly, Angela Seiders, Laura Silverman, Roni Myers-Daub, Sharon Shewbridge, Nicole DeVries, Tania Sotomayor, and Sara Lockett; and all the district's curriculum leaders.
- **Washington Episcopal School** (Maryland) faculty, particularly the essential support from leaders Danny Vogelman, Courtney Clark, Kristin Cuddihy, Mary Lee Nickel, and Zoë Hillman.
- **Waterford Public Schools** (Connecticut) faculty, with special acknowledgment to Craig Powers, Mark Higgins, Kim Podeszwa, and Deryn Winthrop.
- **World of Learning Institute** faculty, specifically Patricia Mulroy and Olivia Grugan, who took our breath away with their early creative designs and commitment to growing storyboards.

Many colleagues and friends deepened our thinking and encouraged us to follow our North Star. Bena Kallick, to whom this book is dedicated, kept us true to the experience of narrative from the student's point of view and provided practical approaches for teachers to generate connections. Marie Hubley Alcock's exceptional strategies for developing learning targets and integrating standards into curriculum maps are an inspiration. Thank you to Donna Rusack, Gail Dahling-Hench, Craig Gastauer, Diane Ullman, and Eric Chagala for your collegiality and contributions to our work. Our gifted graphic designers have created an amazing bank of icons and images that we worked with in all our models. We worked first with Alicia Bamberger, based in Australia, and then with Aaron Roberts, based in the United States, and thank them both for their prompt, imaginative, and professional responses.

ASCD makes our publication possible. We are grateful to Genny Ostertag for her enthusiastic support from the get-go. We thank our lead editor, Katie Martin, whose intelligence, insight, and expertise are a ballast. She understands our ideas and has absolutely made them better with her feedback.

Heidi thanks her husband, Jeffrey, and her family, Rebecca, Gideon, Naomi, Maya, and Matt. She is grateful for their love, support, humor, and encouragement every day.

Allison is buoyed by the love, compassion, humor, and the regular "hip, hip, hoorays" from her husband, Tom, and her children Cuda and Zoe.

Appendix A

Options for Storyboard Components

Composing a storyboard means making choices with a deliberate eye to an audience of students and their families.

Essential Anchor Components

- **Course title with essential question(s) and/or an overview**. Written for the students to promote interest.
- **General time frame.** Typically organized by weeks, months, or marking period.
- **Unit titles.** Framed with compelling language.
- **Visual illustration.** Icons, photographs, or videos.
- **Story focus.** Written in language that is accessible to students and families and describing what students will explore, make sense of, and/or create during each unit.

Other Possible Components

Consider adding any of the following to storyboards you are sharing with colleagues or with students and families.

- **Big-picture goal.** Can be transfer goals (Wiggins & McTighe, 2005) and/or portrait of the graduate goals. *See Episode 2.*
- **Primary standards.** *See Episode 3.*
- **Learning targets.** *See Episode 8.*
- **Authentic assessments.** Can be folded into focus of the story or a stand-alone example. *See Episodes 4 and 7.*
- **Family/student resources.** Links to online content that supports learning at home.

Coaching notes: *Remember the goal is a 10,000-foot view of the course. Too much detail can lessen a storyboard's impact and utility. Ensure that each component is adding to the narrative and works are part of the whole. For example, the title should make sense with illustration that is then elaborated on by the focus of the story.*

Appendix B

How to Introduce Curriculum Storyboards to an Audience

1. **Orientation.** Describe what a curriculum storyboard is and why it matters. *Share key highlights presented in the book, such as*
   - *A curriculum storyboard provides a narrative for the story of the course.*
   - *It is "neurologically friendly"—structured with a beginning, middle, and end.*
   - *It focuses on what students will be actively exploring and doing rather than what teachers will be covering.*
2. **Illustration.** Share ONE curriculum storyboard example with your audience. *Choose one that is accessible to a diverse set of participants due to both content and craftsmanship. Consider any of the following examples in this book:*
   - Figure 4.1: Grade 5 Science
   - Figure 4.2: Algebra I
   - Figure 6.1: The Story of English 1
   - Figure 6.2: Adventure Leadership
   - Figure 7.2: Early Childhood Science
   - Figure 7.3: Geometry
   - Figure 8.2: Survival Spanish
   - Figure 8.4: Grade 1 Reading
   - Figure 9.1: Grade 3 Social Studies
3. **The See, Think, Wonder Protocol.** Walk your audience through a structured analysis of an example storyboard.
   - SEE: *Where does your eye go to first? Where does it go next? What do you notice about the word choice and tone of the storyboard?*
   - THINK: *Who (what audiences) might benefit from seeing this? How might it be used? What other additional information might you like to see on the storyboard?*
   - WONDER: *What are some of the strengths of this design? What are some of the challenges? How would you begin to design something like this?*

Appendix C

Curriculum Storyboard Feedback Form

Developed with Little Elm ISD, Texas

Thank you for taking the time to review and offer feedback and guidance to improve the clarity and accessibility of our curriculum storyboards. We aim for storyboards that provide a 10,000-foot view for students and families of the compelling storyline as they explore designated topics.

As you review each element of the curriculum storyboard, check YES if it meets the criteria **OR** check NOT YET (if it does not) and then provide guidance on what about it, from your perspective, is confusing, missing, or needs improvement.

STORYBOARD ELEMENT	YES	NOT YET	GUIDANCE
Course Title with Essential Questions. • Are essential questions written in clear, accessible (student-friendly) language? • Do they frame student inquiry throughout the course?			
Unit Titles • Are unit titles clear and compelling?			
Image Cues • Do the images help tell the story (connection to titles and focus)? • Do the images represent who students are and/or authentic situations that students will explore?			
Focus of the Story • Is this written in an invitational style, with vocabulary that will be clear and accessible to families and students? • Are there purposeful transitions that highlight the connections among the units? (Example: *We start our journey with ___. Next, we explore ___.*)			
Transfer Goals • Are the subject area transfer goals aligned with the focus of the story?			

Appendix D

Student Prompts to Foster Connections

Developed in collaboration with Bena Kallick

When learners become immersed in making connections and crafting ideas, they reveal more about themselves. The following sample prompts, linked to three Habits of Mind (metacognition, thinking interdependently, and applying past knowledge to new situations) can be adapted to many grade levels and subject areas.

Metacognition

- *What are a few words to describe how you are feeling right now?*
- *What strategies are most helpful to you when you are trying to put yourself in the mood to do some work?*
- *What are the steps you have taken so far as you work? How are you feeling about your progress?*
- *What are some actions you might take to fire up your curiosity and wonderment? How do those actions impact your thinking and imagining?*
- *How are you feeling about what others are saying about your ideas?*
- *How are you receiving what someone else is saying about their own ideas?*

Thinking Interdependently

- *How are you interacting with what someone else is saying about your ideas?*
- *How are you interacting with what someone else is saying about their own ideas?*
- *What are a few words you would like others to use to describe you as a thinker?*
- *What are some ideas you have about this topic (or problem, challenge, issue) that were influenced by the thoughts of others?*
- *What are some conditions that help you have the courage to share your thinking with others?*
- *What are some cues you look for to help you monitor how you are responding to others and how others are responding to you?*

Applying Past Knowledge to New Situations:

- *What do you already know about this topic? Are there experiences in your life that help you in thinking about this topic (or problem, challenge, issue)?*
- *What actions might you take to stimulate your curiosity or fascination for further investigation?*
- *What strategies might you use to broaden your thinking and understand other perspectives?*
- *How has your thinking on this topic (or problem, challenge, issue) changed over time?*

Focus on Learning Sets

A learning set is a streamlined format for the design of learning experiences using clear language, action prompts, and visual cues to engage students. It is an exciting, practical, and dynamic solution to the problem of lesson plan layouts that are packed with many teacher-directed steps that cultivate student dependence.

Learning sets help teachers to . . .

- Create a storyline and narrative arc of the learning experience.
- Ensure that the actions align to the goal of the unit, course, and school.
- Identify the critical steps students must take to meet the learning target.
- Eliminate non-essential information.
- Visually represent the type of action students will take.
- Review RANGE learning experience types to ensure variety. *For example, if we notice nothing but reading and quiz icons throughout a week's plan, we can rethink to expand the possibilities.*

Learning sets help students to . . .

- Preview the range of learning experiences scanning the iconography and brief, clear, and accessible statements.
- Become more self-directed and connected to the learning experience.

Review the sample learning set here. Can you point to the following elements?

- Clear and accessible language
- A balance of a big-picture view and details
- A range of assignments that are diverse in form and type
- Phrasing that positions students to be self-directed learners

Learning Set: Personal Logo Design

Developed By: Aaron Roberts

TIME FRAME	9 Days

SCHOOL	Mason High School

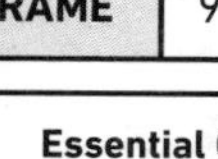

Essential Question(s): How can colors and symbols combine to create a logo that reflects my personal values and interests? How can I apply research and feedback from others to refine and improve my logo design?

Goals: Reflect on your personal values and how they might be represented in a simple, easy-to-understand logo.

Create a logo via hand drawing techniques and then on vector-based drawing software.

Overview: A logo is a visual representation of a company or organization and is an important part of their branding. It is essential to create a logo that is unique, memorable, and eye-catching. A successful logo should incorporate elements of the company's values and mission. For example, the Nike logo represents a feeling of quickness and athleticism. During this logo project, you will explore various existing logos and then create one for yourself! You will need to reflect on your own values before brainstorming and sketching. With careful planning and a little creativity, you can create a logo that you will be proud to share with the world.

	LEARNING TARGET	ENGAGE	EXAMINE	DEMONSTRATE
EPISODE 1	I can explore a world full of logos and identify how they express a company's values. I can critique a logo design by analyzing how well it communicates a company's or team's values.	In small groups, **identify** 10 logos that the group can agree are eye-catching. Then, **revise** your list by narrowing it down to three logos that your team finds especially remarkable.	**Collaborate** to research the corporate or team values, mission, or vision statements associated with the logo. - Discuss to what extent your research is reflected in the logo. - Label the logo with the symbols, colors, or fonts that communicate the values, vision, or mission. 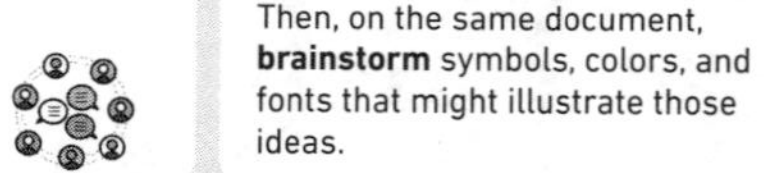	**Reflect** on the things that you personally value. Create a document with a list of words, phrases, Habits of Mind, attitudes, or mindsets that are important to you. Then, on the same document, **brainstorm** symbols, colors, and fonts that might illustrate those ideas.
EPISODE 2	I can apply my research by sketching, brainstorming, and refining logo design ideas.	**Watch** the Aaron Draplin logo design video to get a view of his creative process. While watching, consider how many variations of a single idea he tried before settling into a final design.	Considering your reflections from Episode 1, **brainstorm** and **sketch** a page of simple logo designs. Each design should, in some way, illustrate your personal values or interests. 	**Draw and present to a small group of peers** one page of quick logo sketches. Describe to them which logo ideas are your favorites. Ask them how they see the logo representing your values. Consider any refinements to your design. 
EPISODE 3	I can create a fully vector logo much like professional designers do.	**Watch** the provided videos, the demonstrations in class, or **explore** Adobe Illustrator on your own to learn the basics of vector drawing.	Paste a photo or a scan of your best drawings into a new Illustrator document. Create your first **prototype** by tracing your works. Then, add innovations like new or more refined shapes, fonts, and varying colors to better express your personality. 	Complete your vector logo and **present** two variations of the base design on a single artboard. Print them as a sticker that can be used to show off your work. Finally, **consider** how else you might present your logo. Social media? In your email signature?

References

Australian Curriculum, Assessment, and Reporting Authority (ACARA). (2022). Australian Curriculum. https://www.australiancurriculum.edu.au/

Big Picture Learning Australia. (n.d.). What is the International Big Picture Learning Credential? https://www.bigpicture.org.au/what-international-big-picture-learning-credential

Campbell, K. K., Huzman, S. S., & Burkholder, T. A. (2015). *The rhetorical act: Thinking, speaking, and writing critically* (5th ed.). Cengage Learning.

Childs Elementary School. (n.d.). What are the PYP key concepts? www.mccsc.edu/page/3945

Creswell, J. (1997). *Creating worlds, constructing meaning: The Scottish storyline method.* Heinemann.

Cron, L. (2012). *Wired for story: The writer's guide to using brain science to hook readers from the very first sentence.* Ten Speed Press.

Cron, L. (2013). Forget theme! Instead ask, "And so, what's my point?" https://writerunboxed.com/2013/12/12/forget-theme-instead-ask-and-so-whats-my-point

Definitions.net. (n.d.). What does film editing mean? https://www.definitions.net/definition/film+editing),

Dietiker, L. (2013). Mathematical texts as narrative: Rethinking curriculum. *For the Learning of Mathematics, 33*(3), 14–19.

Dreyfuss, H. (1955). *Designing for people.* Simon & Schuster.

Finch, C. (1995). *The art of Walt Disney: From Mickey Mouse to the Magic Kingdoms.* Abrams.

Finerman, G. (2022). Hinsdale high schooler uses school program to revamp baseball field. WMUR News 9. http://www.wmur.com/article/hinsdale-nh-high-schooler-uses-school-program-to-revamp-baseball-field/39804956

Goyal, N. (2016). *Schools on trial: How freedom and creativity can fix our educational malpractice.* Doubleday.

Habits of Mind Institute. (2016). Transfer goals. https://www.habitsofmindinstitute.org/wp-content/uploads/2016/08/TRANSFER-GOALS.pdf

Halinen, I. (2018). The new educational curriculum in Finland. In M. Matthes, L. Pulkkinen, C. Clouder, & B. Heys (Eds.), *Improving the quality of childhood in Europe, Vol. 7* (pp. 75–89). Alliance for Childhood European Network Foundation.

Holston, S. (2019). Why I'm learning neuroscience through stories. *The Startup*. https://medium.com/swlh/why-im-learning-neuroscience-through-stories-be8b17a9a773

Jacobs, H. H. (1989). *Interdisciplinary curriculum: Design and implementation*. ASCD.

Jacobs, H. H. (2002). Integrated curriculum design. In J. T. Klein (Ed.), *Interdisciplinary education K–12 and college: A foundation for K–16 dialogue*. The College Board.

Jacobs, H. H. (Ed.). (2004). *Getting results with curriculum mapping*. ASCD.

Jacobs, H. H., & Alcock, M. A. (2017). *Bold moves for schools: How we create remarkable learning environments*. ASCD.

Jacobs, H. H., & Johnson, A. (2009). *The curriculum mapping planner: Templates, tools, and resources for effective professional development*. ASCD.

Jacobs, H. H., & Zmuda, A. (2021, December). Streamlined lesson planning for learner engagement. *Educational Leadership, 79*(4), 44–49.

Jacobs, H. H., & Zmuda, A. (2023, February). Storyboarding our curriculum. *Educational Leadership, 80*(5), 22–27.

Jacobs, H. H., & Zmuda, A. (n.d.). Curriculum as narrative. https://learnings.ets.com/3-part-process-for-making-deliberate-curriculum-choices

Kallick, B., & Zmuda, A. (2017). *Students at the center: Personalized learning with Habits of Mind*. ASCD.

Kavanagh, S., & Ojalgo, H. E. (2012, January 24). On the stump: Examining the form and function of campaign speeches. *New York Times*. https://archive.nytimes.com/learning.blogs.nytimes.com/2012/01/24/on-the-stump-examining-the-form-and-function-of-campaign-speeches/

Kelly, D. (n.d.). Why do our brains demand a narrative? *Headspace*. https://www.headspace.com/articles/brains-demand-narrative

Khadem, R., & Khadem, L. (2017). *Total alignment: Tools and tactics for streamlining your organization*. Entrepreneur Media.

Littky, D., & Grabelle, S. (2004). *The big picture: Education is everyoney's business*. ASCD.

Martinez-Conde, S., Alexander, R. G., Blum, D., Britton, N., Lipska, B. K., Quirk, G. J., Swiss, J. I., Willems, R. M., & Macknik, S. L. (2019). The storytelling brain: How neuroscience stories help bridge the gap between research and society. *Journal of Neuroscience, 39*(42), 8285–8290.

McMurray, C. (2021, March 4). Why the brain loves stories. BrainFacts.org. https://www.brainfacts.org/neuroscience-in-society/the-arts-and-the-brain/2021/why-the-brain-loves-stories-030421

McTighe, J., & Wiggins, G. (2013). *Essential questions: Opening doors to understanding*. ASCD.

McTighe, J., & Willis, J. (2019). *Upgrade your teaching: Understanding by Design meets neuroscience*. ASCD.

Merlino, F. J. (2022, October 7). *STEM: Preparing future problem solvers*. https://www.openaccessgovernment.org/wp-content/uploads/2022/10/openaccessgovernment.org-STEM-Preparing-future-problem-solvers.pdf

Merriam-Webster. (n.d.). Pitch. In *Merriam-Webster.com dictionary*. www.merriam-webster.com/dictionary/pitch

Merriam-Webster. (n.d.). Streamline. In *Merriam-Webster.com dictionary*. www.merriam-webster.com/dictionary/streamline

Neeley, L., Barker, E., Bayer, S., Maktoufi, R., Wu, K.J., & Zaringhalam, M/. (2020, June). Linking scholarship and practice: Narrative and identity in science. *Frontiers in Communication, 5*. https://doi.org/10.3389/fcomm.2020.00035

Newman, K. M. (2016, May 27). A simple story can improve students' grades in science. *Greater Good Magazine*. https://greatergood.berkeley.edu/article/item/a_simple_story_can_improve_students_grades_in_science

OECD. (2019). *PISA 2018 assessment and analytical framework*. Author. https://doi.org/10.1787/b25efab8-en.

Olson, R. (2015). *Houston, we have a narrative: Why science needs story*. University of Chicago Press.

Online Etymology Dictionary. (n.d.). Streamline. https://www.etymonline.com/search?q=streamline&utm_campaign=sd&utm_medium=serp&utm_source=ds_search

Peters, B. G. (2018, March 21). 6 rules of great storytelling as told by Pixar. https://medium.com/@Brian_G_Peters/6-rules-of-great-storytelling-as-told-by-pixar-fcc6ae225f50

Plenge, A., & Pilgreen, T. (2023). Reinventing the mall. *Dialogue, 35*. https://www.gensler.com/publications/dialogue/35/reinventing-the-mall

Poon-McGovern, E. (n.d.). *Dragons vs. elephants storyline*. https://www.storyline.org/articles/dragons-vs-elephants-storyline

Quinn, M. (2020, May 6). What makes a great pitch. *Harvard Business Review*. https://hbr.org/2020/05/what-makes-a-great-pitch

Renken, E. (2020, April 11). How stories connect and persuade us: Unleashing the brain power of narrative. Shots: Health News from NPR. https://www.npr.org/sections/health-shots/2020/04/11/815573198/how-stories-connect-and-persuade-us-unleashing-the-brain-power-of-narrative

Richmond, A. S. (2016, September). Constructing a learner-centered syllabus: One professor's journey (IDEA Paper #60). Idea Center. https://www.ideaedu.org/Portals/0/Uploads/Documents/IDEA%20Papers/IDEA%20Papers/PaperIDEA_60.pdf

Sahlberg, P. (2015, October 5). Do teachers in Finland have more autonomy? *The Conversation*. https://theconversation.com/do-teachers-in-finland-have-more-autonomy-48371

Sapega, M. (2021, September 15). What is a storyboard? Your ultimate storyboarding guide. *CareerFoundry Blog*. https://careerfoundry.com/en/blog/ui-design/what-is-a-storyboard/#what-is-a-storyboard

Schlesinger, L. A., Kiefer, C. F., & Brown, P. B. (2012, March 21). What to do when you don't know what to do. *Harvard Business Review*. https://hbr.org/2012/03/what-to-do-when-you-dont-know

ScienceDaily. (2011, January 18). Storytelling may help control blood pressure in African-Americans. https://www.sciencedaily.com/releases/2011/01/110118113151.htm

Scottish Consultative Council on the Curriculum. (n.d.). What is the Scottish storyline method? https://www.storyline.org/

Smith, J. A. (2016, August 25). The science of the story. *Berkeley Blog*. https://news.berkeley.edu/berkeley_blog/the-science-of-the-story

STEM Egypt. (n.d.). Egypt grand challenges. https://sites.google.com/a/stemegypt.edu.eg/2015/Present-and-Justify-a-Problem-and-Solution-Requirements/egypt-grand-challenge

Suttie, J. (2015, May 12). How our bodies react to seeing goodness. *Greater Good Magazine*. https://greatergood.berkeley.edu/article/item/how_our_bodies_react_human_goodness

Tharp, T. (2011). *The creative habit: Learn it and use it for life*. Simon & Schuster.

United Nations Development Programme. (n.d.). What are the sustainable development goals? https://www.undp.org/sustainable-development-goals

Wagner, T., & Dintersmith, T. (2015)). *Most likely to succeed: Preparing our kids for the future*. Scribner.

Whitman, G., & Kelleher, I. (2016). *Neuroteach: Brain science and the future of education*. Rowman & Littlefield.

Wiggins, G. (1989, May). A true test: Toward more authentic and equitable assessment. *Phi Delta Kappan, 70*(9), 703–713. https://grantwiggins.files.wordpress.com/2014/01/wiggins-atruetest-kappan89.pdf

Wiggins, G. & McTighe, J. (2005). *Understanding by Design: Expanded 2nd edition*. ASCD.

Willis, J. (2017, September 12). The neuroscience of narrative and memory. *Edutopia*. https://www.edutopia.org/article/neuroscience-narrative-and-memory

Yalanska, M. (2016, May 23). Iconic simplicity: The vital role of icons [Blog post]. *Tubik* https://blog.tubikstudio.com/iconic-simplicity-the-vital-role-of-icons/

Zak, P. (2015, January/February). Why inspiring stories make us react: The neuroscience of narrative. *Cerebrum*. https://www.ncbi.nlm.nih.gov/pmc/articles/PMC4445577

Zmuda, A. G. (n.d.). Real challenges—in every sense of the word. *Learning Personalized*. https://www.learningpersonalized.com/real-challenges-in-every-sense-of-the-word

Zmuda, A. G., & Tomaino, M. (2001). *The competent classroom*. Teachers College Press.

Index

The letter *f* following a page locator denotes a figure.

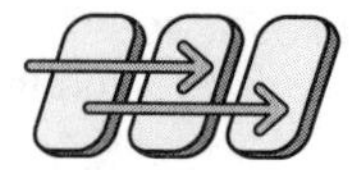

About the Authors

Heidi Hayes Jacobs works with schools, organizations, and agencies to create responsive learning environments, upgrade curriculum, and support teaching strategies to meet the needs of contemporary learners. Her models of curriculum mapping and her design and approach to modernizing school ecosystems and learning spaces have been featured in numerous books, articles, podcasts, and software solutions throughout the world.

Through her collaboration with the brilliant Allison Zmuda, Heidi has become fascinated by the possibilities storyboarding offers to streamline curriculum and increase student-facing engagement. She can be reached at heidi@curriculum21.com, @heidihayesjacob, or https://www.linkedin.com/in/heidihayesjacobs/

Allison Zmuda is a longstanding education consultant focused on curriculum development with an emphasis on personalized learning. Just as she advocates for personalized learning to be used *by* her clients, she practices it when engaging *with* her clients.

Allison continues to benefit from collaborative partnerships: most notably, coauthorship of 12 books, curation of *Learning Personalized,* codirection of the Institute for Habits of Mind, and cocreator of curriculum storyboards with the inspirational Heidi Hayes Jacobs. She can be reached at allison@allisonzmuda.com, @allison_zmuda, or https://www.linkedin.com/in/allisonzmuda/

Related ASCD Resources: Curriculum and Lesson Planning

At the time of publication, the following resources were available (ASCD stock numbers in parentheses).

Better Learning Through Structured Teaching: A Framework for the Gradual Release of Responsibility, 3rd Edition by Douglas Fisher and Nancy Frey (#121031)

Curriculum 21: Essential Education for a Changing World by Heidi Hayes Jacobs (Ed.) (#109008)

Designed to Learn: Using Design Thinking to Bring Purpose and Passion to the Classroom by Lindsay Portnoy (#120026)

Ensuring High-Quality Curriculum: How to Design, Revise, or Adopt Curriculum Aligned to Student Success by Angela Di Michele Lalor (#116006)

Improving Student Learning One Teacher at a Time, 2nd Edition by Jane E. Pollock and Laura J. Tolone (#117013)

Making Curriculum Matter: How to Build SEL, Equity, and Other Priorities into Daily Instruction by Angela Di Michele Lalor (#122007)

Rigor by Design, Not Chance: Deeper Thinking Through Actionable Instruction and Assessment by Karin Hess (#122036)

Students at the Center: Personalized Learning with Habits of Mind by Bena Kallick and Allison Zmuda (#117015)

Teaching for Deeper Learning: Tools to Engage Students in Meaning Making by Jay McTighe and Harvey F. Silver (#120022)

Teaching with Clarity: How to Prioritize and Do Less So Students Understand More by Tony Frontier (#121015)

Tell Your Story: Teaching Students to Become World-Changing Thinkers and Writers by Pam Allyn and Ernest Morrell (#122031)

Understanding by Design, Expanded 2nd Edition by Grant Wiggins and Jay McTighe (#103055)

The Understanding by Design Guide to Creating High-Quality Units by Grant Wiggins and Jay McTighe (#109107)

Where Great Teaching Begins: Planning for Student Thinking and Learning by Anne R. Reeves (#111023)

For up-to-date information about ASCD resources, go to www.ascd.org. You can search the complete archives of *Educational Leadership* at www.ascd.org/el. To contact us, send an email to member@ascd.org or call 1-800-933-2723 or 703-578-9600.